DEAR CHURCH

A PARAPHRASE OF GOD'S LETTERS TO HIS PEOPLE

GABRIEL MILLER

ALL PEOPLES MINISTRIES
LYNCHBURG, VA

Dear Church: A Paraphrase of God's Letters to His People

Published by All Peoples Ministries
P.O. Box 3034
Lynchburg, Virginia 24503
www.allpeoplesministries.org

Copyright © 2020 Gabriel Miller

All rights reserved. This book is protected by the copyright laws of the United States of America. This book may not be copied or reprinted for commercial gain or profit.

Cover design by Samuel C. Petty

Scripture quotations marked (NKJV) are taken from the Holy Bible, New King James Version®. Copyright © 1982 by Thomas Nelson, Inc. Used by permission. All rights reserved.

Scripture quotations marked (NIV) are taken from the Holy Bible, New International Version®, NIV®. Copyright © 1973, 1978, 1984, 2011 by Biblica, Inc.™ Used by permission of Zondervan. All rights reserved worldwide. www.zondervan.com The "NIV" and "New International Version" are trademarks registered in the United States Patent and Trademark Office by Biblica, Inc.™

ISBN: 978-0-9987608-7-2

Printed in the United States of America

To Dad, a student and teacher of the Word

CONTENTS

INTRODUCTION

Imagine opening your mailbox to find a letter from God. I know, impossible. But what if it happened? What if God decided to communicate directly with you, revealing pieces of His identity, laying out the specifics of His rescue plan for humanity, correcting you where you're wrong, and encouraging you where you're right? Well, He's actually done that already.

The Epistles are unique among the Bible's literary forms. Whereas the Old Testament, the Gospels, the Acts, and the Revelation, were written primarily to *inform* their readers; the Epistles were written primarily to *instruct* their readers.

The Epistles also have a unique target audience. The whole Bible was written for the benefit of everyone. But different sections were written toward specific people groups. The Old Testament was written for the Jewish community, and the Gospels and Acts were written for the benefit of a lost and dying world, but the Epistles (and the Revelation) are the only books of the Bible that were specifically written *to* the Church of Jesus Christ. Well ... sort of. Five of the epistles—1 & 2 Timothy, Titus, Philemon, and 3 John—were written to individual Christians. The remaining 16 letters—Hebrews, 1 & 2 John, James, Romans, Galatians, Ephesians, Colossians, Philippians, 1 & 2 Corinthians, 1 & 2 Thessalonians, 1 & 2 Peter, and Jude—were written either to specific regional churches or to the Church-universal. These are the 16 letters we might describe as "God's Letters to His People." And these are the 16 letters that you will find in this book.

Why Paraphrase the Scriptures?

"In your own words, _____." Did you ever get a question like that on a test? You read a passage and then the teacher wanted you to restate that passage in your own words? Or the teacher lectured on World War II, and then wanted you to write an essay on the content of the lecture "in your own words?" Why? Because when you take in information, process it internally, and then restate that information, not parroted, but reshaped, you gain a true understanding of the information.

As I worked through this project, one of the most important things to me was to make sure that I had thoroughly processed and comprehended everything I was reading in the Scriptures. I recommend this task to everyone. Are you having trouble understanding a particular passage? Read it over and over. Read it in as many translations as you can find. Read what's before it and what's after it. Connect all the dots in your mind. And then restate it in your own words. (Notice, that's not the same thing as twisting it to say something else that you want it to say.) I firmly believe the Bible was not meant to be an enigma. There are some difficult passages. And depending on the translation, there can sometimes be tough sledding in the grammar and writing style. But at its core, the message of the Bible is not elusive; it is plain enough for everyone to comprehend.

I hope this book will help you to comprehend it. I hope that as people read it, they will move closer to a deep and rich understanding of the message God is wanting to communicate.

How to Use this Paraphrase

First of all, it is important to keep in mind that what you are about to read is *not* the infallible Word of God. It is one man's paraphrase of the infallible Word of God. And since it's a man's paraphrase, it is likely fallible. I don't pretend that there's no possibility of error. But I do, with great sobriety, affix my stamp of approval on what I have written here. With all my heart I believe I have captured the essence of what the biblical authors were really saying. One of the questions I kept in mind throughout this process was, "If I were taking dictation for this biblical author, would he challenge or change what I have written?" Would he say, "No, that's not what I'm saying"? Would he say, "Yes, that's exactly what I meant"? Or would he say, "Well that's not exactly what I said, but it precisely captures the spirit of what I'm getting at"?

With that in mind, my recommendation is that you use this book as a supplement to your daily Bible reading, not as a substitute for a good translation. Read an entire letter in one sitting if possible. Read the paraphrase, then read a translation, then reread the paraphrase, then read another translation. Read the paraphrase side-by-side with a good translation. (I recommend reading a mix of NKJV, NIV, NLT, CSB, and NASB to develop a clear sense of any passage.) Find all of the places where I have taken liberties with the order, and with the language. Ask yourself: why? Read critically but not cynically. Decide for yourself if the paraphrase does the text justice. If you read this way, the Bible will "click" for many of you in ways you never imagined.

In addition, use the discussion questions to help you deeply process the Word. The book is great for individual devotion, but it is also intended for small-group (or even congregational) study, featuring a 20-week reading plan. The pace amounts to less than one chapter per day.

What to Expect

I think you'll find that this paraphrase is quite a bit different from popular translations and even other paraphrases. I was not afraid, in some cases, to make fairly wide departures from the actual text, in order to bring its meaning to life. The result is a version of the Bible that, I believe, has achieved these objectives:

1. Ensure readability
2. Provide structure to aid comprehension
3. Illuminate vague passages
4. Represent ideas accurately

5. Infuse a homiletic complexion

6. Contextualize appropriately for modern readers

- *Ensure Readability*

I have been careful to ensure that the paraphrase is readable. This means that I took some liberties with sentence structure. In some places I even took liberties with paragraph structure or chapter structure. Ensuring readability does not mean that I shied away from big words, however. Nor did I always smooth out technical theological terminology. So, instead of trying to dumb down words like *propitiation*, for example, I simply clarified the word's meaning, in and around its usage.

- *Provide Structure to Aid Comprehension*

I have added some linguistic scaffolding to the letters, in order to provide readers with an obvious organizational plan that will help them retain the message. This looks different for different letters. For example, Romans has amazing structure already; this I merely worked to accentuate. The structure of Hebrews is less obvious, though still present; and in that case I superimposed some structure without damaging the meaning. In the case of James (which, in the original text opens rather abruptly, diving right into instruction in Verse 2), I simply added a buffer paragraph that makes it actually read like a letter:

[v. 1]	Greetings ...
[added buffer]	I have several things on my heart to share with you. I can say with confidence that what I am writing to you today is directly from the Lord and extremely important, so please take note.
[v. 2]	First, you need to ...

- *Illuminate Vague Passages*

The Epistles are mostly straight-forward, as compared with, say, the Revelation. Still, a few places, particularly in Paul's writings, leave most of us scratching our heads. For example, what did he mean by "from now on, we regard no one according to the flesh" (2Co 5:16; NKJV)? Or "they are not all Israel who are of Israel" (Rom 9:6; NKJV)? Or "firstborn over all creation" and "firstborn from the dead" (Col 1:15,18; NKJV)? I have attempted to render these kinds of puzzling phrases with clarity.

- *Represent Ideas Accurately*

The key word here is *ideas*. For the most part, I am not concerned with representing each Greek word accurately. (That is called *translation*, and one would presumably need to be a Greek scholar in order to take on that project.) Instead, I have done my best to represent the author's (and hence, God's) *ideas* accurately. Sometimes that means getting across an idea at the phrase or sentence level. Sometimes that means getting an idea across at the paragraph level. Sometimes that means getting an idea across at the "chapter" level or higher. In more than one place, I changed the order of paragraphs in order to communicate the bigger-picture idea.

In some select cases, on the other hand, I have offered translations of single words. I regularly looked up the Greek words in various lexicons in order to get a true sense of the meaning, and in some cases, I chose to translate certain words differently from any translation I came across. This is true of virtually all the items in the "to-don't list" passages, for example, such as Romans 1:29-31, 13:13; Galatians 5:19-21; Ephesians 5:3-4; and Colossians 3:5.

- *Infuse a Homiletic Complexion*

I believe the Bible makes the best sermon. It preaches itself if you take the time to listen. A paraphrase should not be thought of as an infraction of the warning in Revelation 22:19, "And if anyone takes away from the words of the book ... God shall take away his part from the Book of Life" (NKJV). Rather, it should be understood as a first-layer sermon on Scripture. A preacher begins with Scripture and extrapolates. A paraphrase similarly begins with Scripture and extrapolates. I want this paraphrase not merely to be read by the reader but to preach to the reader.

- *Contextualize Appropriately for Modern Readers*
    A paraphrase is also the first, closest layer of interpretation. My paraphrase is not meant to be richly interpretive, but I am under no illusion that my theology won't be reflected in it. That's simply the nature of the beast. For the average reader, any hint of theological bias will breeze right by. More advanced theologians will be able to draw conclusions about my views, I'm sure.

One of the most obvious ways in which my hermeneutic will express itself is in those passages for which I have made major compromises to the literal meaning of the text for the sake of targeting the modern English-speaking audience. As a rule, those passages that I believe address culturally-specific issues in regional first-century churches, I have modified to present an equivalent, theologically valid passage for the modern English reader. For example, instructions to slaves and masters have been modified to address employees and employers. And in the case of 1 Corinthians 11, the mysterious "hair" and "head covering" references, which are clearly problems Paul is addressing within the Corinthian culture, have been completely reshaped. We don't know precisely what Paul was getting at here, but Craig Blomberg has astutely affirmed what we do know: "What all these phenomena share is that Paul was concerned that Christian men and women at worship not appear as though they were either religiously unfaithful to God or sexually unfaithful to their spouses."* This was my guiding thought in the paraphrase process for that passage.

---

* Craig Blomberg, "Women in Ministry: A Complementarian Perspective," in *Two Views on Women in Ministry*, ed. Stanley N. Gundry (Grand Rapids: Zondervan, 2005), 157.

A Word About the Order of the Letters

The letters that follow are arranged neither canonically nor chronologically. My primary thought in presenting them in this order was that I wanted the modern reader to be first struck with high Christology, and then branch out from there. Thus, Hebrews comes first, followed by 1 John (in particular, Chapter 1). I wanted to include Colossians 1 there as well, but it seemed more appropriate to nestle it in with the rest of Paul's letters. Going on from there, James and Romans were purposely paired together, as were Romans and Galatians, and Ephesians and Colossians. The letters to the Thessalonians, with their strong end-times messages, were placed in closest proximity to Peter and Jude.

Dear Reader

It's time to dig in. As you begin to read *Dear Church*, know that you, my spiritual brothers and sisters, are dear to me. I hope our Father will use this work to encourage and inspire you. I believe He will.

THE LETTER TO THE BELIEVING
HEBREWS

1 God spoke to earlier generations of saints through His prophets. Now, He is speaking to us through His Son. Who is this Son? How does He compare to other important figures in the Bible? And what is it that He does for us that is so significant? These are questions that will be answered in this letter. First, let's take note of six important facts about the Son. We will continue to reference them throughout our discussion.

The Son is the *Maker of all things* and the *Heir of all things*. God made the world through Him, and God has given the world as an inheritance to Him. The Son is also the *Extension of the Father* and the *Sustainer of all things*. And the way that the Son sustains the world is by speaking over it. To look at the Son is to see the reflection of the Father in a mirror. In one sense you would say you are technically not looking at the Father, but rather the *reflection* of the Father. In another sense you *are* looking at the Father; you're certainly not looking at someone else. That's how integrated the Son and the Father are. The Son is the Father's exact image. Furthermore, the Son is the *Purifier of the believers*, cleansing us from sin; after He completed His mission of purification, He assumed His role as *King over all things*. (That is, all of the authority of God the Father has been given to the Son.)

It should be obvious already that the Son is superior to the angels. All the more so when we realize that God said things to Jesus that He never said to any angel. Things like, "You are My Son, I am Your Father," and "Let all of the angels worship Him," and, "Sit at My right hand until I crush your enemies and prop Your feet up with them." (Now, "sitting at God's right hand" is a figurative way of saying that the Son has been given all of the authority of the Father.) By contrast, God speaks of "sending the angels out as servants." They are merely servants sent by God to minister to us who will inherit salvation. He also says to the Son, "You laid the foundation of the earth from the very beginning, O Lord. You made the heavens. All of creation will pass away, but You will never pass away." In another place God says to the Son, "You, O God, have an eternal throne and a righteous scepter. You love what is right and hate what is wrong, O God. That's why Your God has anointed You above all others." He actually calls Him "God!" That's because the Son is fully divine!

2 Well then, it becomes critical that we get a firm grasp on everything we have heard from the Son and about the Son, so that we don't drift away from the faith. If the things God spoke through angels were binding, and people were punished for disobedience to those words, how much greater will our demise be if we neglect to fully embrace the message of salvation that God has spoken through His Son? This message was even confirmed to us by Spiritual gifts, signs and wonders, and miracles of all sorts!

It wasn't angels that God made the world subject to; it was the Son. The Scriptures say:

> Who are we as people that You, God, should even give
> us a thought, much less take care of us the way You do?
> And yet You have made us a little lower than the angels,
> crowned us with glory and honor, and put us in charge
> of the rest of Your creation, subjecting it to us.

Of course, not everything was subject to us at that point. No, Jesus has gone before us to make this prophecy a reality. It is He who was made lower than the angels for a short time; it was He who suffered death, crowned with glory and honor; it was He who took our punishment upon Himself. In so doing, He has become the rightful Heir to all of God's authority. And the authority that He has, He has delegated to us. (All of this was made possible by His suffering. This makes sense when you think about it. Somebody had to suffer, and He was the only One qualified to suffer in our place.)

Now we who are being made holy are in complete unity with the Son. He's not ashamed to call us His brothers, declaring, "Father, I will testify about You to My brothers. I will sing Your praises right along with them when they get together to have church." He also said this: "I will trust in You, and so will the children You have given Me."

Let's take a minute to explain why the Son had to become human, because that's an important concept. There are two reasons why the Son had to become human. The first is that if He had remained divine-only, it would have been impossible for Him to die. Since death was the price of our redemption, He had to become human so that He could die. By dying He defeated the devil at his own game, death. Now we have been set free from the power of death. One day we will rise in glory just as He did!

The second reason He had to become human was that *we* are human. It was necessary for the One who served as our substitute to be like us in every respect. He didn't become an angel, because He wasn't trying to rescue angels. He came to rescue us! Because He was human, He was able to bear the sin of humanity. Indeed, because He was tempted in all of the same categories of sin we are tempted in, He is able to help us overcome our temptations. So, you see, in order for the Son to be qualified to serve as our ultimate High Priest, appeasing the wrath of God on our behalf by His own self-sacrifice, He had to be both *fully God* and *fully human!*

3 Now that we've considered Jesus' identity as the God-man, let's consider some particulars of His relationship to us, namely: (1) the way He delivers us from bondage into our eternal inheritance, (2) the way He empowers us to persevere to the end, and (3) the way He cleanses us through and through and brings our salvation to its completion and finality.

First, think about how Jesus compares to Moses. Jesus was faithful in His mission, just as Moses was faithful in his. God entrusted His people to Moses, His servant. Now God has entrusted His people to Jesus, His Son. In a sense, His people are His "house," in that they are His dwelling place. But Jesus is worthy of more glory than Moses, because Jesus actually built the house, whereas Moses was merely a part of the house. Moses delivered God's people out of Egypt, but he was not able to complete his mission by leading them into the Promised Land. Jesus is a better Deliverer than Moses, since He is not only able to deliver us *from* bondage but is also able to deliver us *into* all that God has promised. As the *Maker of all things*, Jesus has *made* a way for us to be free from sin; and as the *Heir of all things*, Jesus has secured our *inheritance*.

In response, the Holy Spirit is speaking the same warning to us that He spoke to the saints of the past:

God is calling you today. Don't harden your hearts and rebel as they did in the wilderness. They saw Me do the miraculous for forty years, and yet they still inclined themselves away from Me and never came to truly know Me. So I swore in righteous anger that they would never enter My rest.

I'm warning you, brothers and sisters. Don't allow a sliver of unbelief to creep in and slowly turn you away from God. Everyone should be reminding everyone else of this warning daily, so that nobody becomes deceived and hardened by sin. We'll all be able to share in Christ's inheritance if we continue to cling to the pure faith all the way to the end. There's still time. It's still "today." So listen to His voice, and obey.

Think about it. Who was it that rebelled? With whom was God angry? Whose corpses were strewn in the wilderness? To whom was God referring when He said, "They will never enter My rest"? It was those who sinned, those who disobeyed. Thus, they could not enter because of their unbelief. Don't you see? Unbelief in the heart results in disobedient actions, but faith in the heart results in obedient actions. Church, you must trust and obey to obtain the inheritance!

4 Now, the promise of rest still remains today. Even Joshua didn't lead the people into God's final rest (though he was able to lead them into the Promised Land). We know this because God spoke of another day of rest yet to come after the conquest of the Promised Land. So, Jesus is a better Overcomer than Joshua, since He is not only able to ensure our inheritance, but is also able to lead us to God's rest. As the *Extension of the Father* and the *Sustainer of all things*, Jesus empowers us to persevere to the end, where rest awaits. This is His ministry of endurance to us.

So, the promise of rest remains. And we ought to quake in our boots at the thought of missing it. The Gospel was preached to them, and the Gospel was preached to us. The only reason it took root in us was because we seized it by faith, whereas they did not. The only ones who will enter His rest are those who believe. To the ones who didn't believe, He angrily promised, "They won't enter My rest." But God had already established this rest from the beginning, as the Scripture says, "He rested on the seventh day." The first candidates for His rest failed to find it because they disobeyed Him. So He designated another day for another group of candidates to enter His rest. That day is today, and that group of candidates is you! So, in the words of David, I repeat, "Don't harden your hearts! Listen and obey!"

Now, to enter *His* rest, *you* have to rest. You have to stop trying to do everything yourself and let Him take care of it all. So, let's do everything within our power to rest in Him. If we don't, if we disobey as the Israelites did, there's no way we'll make it! Don't you know that the Lord knows your heart better than you know it yourself? The Word of God is alive and extremely energetic. He slices through to the core, exposing every thought and motive. Nothing is hidden from Him! You will give an account one day!

So hold on to the faith until the end! There's no reason you can't do it. Jesus delivers and Jesus empowers. Because He is fully God, He is willing and able to give you the strength to endure. And because He is fully man, He is able to sympathize with all of our weaknesses, having been tempted in all the same areas, without faltering. Through our High Priest, God will give you all the mercy you need to help you through any situation, if you will posture yourself for it. So fall down before His throne and expect to receive.

5 Not only does Jesus deliver us from bondage, secure our inheritance, and sustain us to the end; He is also able to close the deal on our salvation. That's because He is a High Priest like we've never seen before. Aaron's priesthood was established to give the Israelites a way to be made right with God. The gifts and sacrifices that the high priest offered on behalf of the people appeased a God who cannot abide any unholiness. But this system was neither permanent nor comprehensive. Jesus is a better Mediator than Aaron, since He is not only able to cleanse us from sin, but also is able to carry through to completion the entire finished work of salvation from sin, imputation of righteousness, and establishment of glorification.

As the *Purifier of all believers,* Jesus has cleansed us from all unrighteousness, even cleansing us down to our consciences. As the *King over all things,* Jesus has the authority to pronounce the finality of our salvation; the entire process is accomplished in Him; His kingship seals the effectiveness of His work.

Those of Aaron's priesthood were *called* to that work. They could not have chosen themselves. They were men chosen by God to serve as representatives of their fellow man, offering gifts and sacrifices on their behalf. Since they, too, were sinful, they had to offer sacrifices for themselves before offering on behalf of the others. They were able to sympathize with the weaknesses of the people because they were also prone to temptation.

Jesus was chosen by God for His priesthood as well. God not only said, "You are My Son," but also proclaimed, "You will forever be a Priest of the same type as Melchizedek." (We'll explain more about this special priesthood of Melchizedek in a moment.) Throughout His time on earth, the Son obeyed the Father without exception, even though that sometimes meant great persecution. He cried out to His Father in the middle of that pain, and His cries were heard because of the fear of God in His heart. Through His obedience He was given the authority to orchestrate the salvation of everyone else who obeys.

There's a lot more we would like to say about this, but you're too spiritually dense to understand it. By this point you should be so well versed in the finer points of the Christian faith that you should be able to teach others. But no, we have to keep sticking the baby bottle in your mouth. You're not mature enough for solid spiritual food.

6 Nevertheless, let's move on from the basics—you don't need more teachings about repentance, faith, baptism, the laying on of hands, the resurrection of the dead, and the eternal judgment. So, God willing, let's go deeper.

Anybody who sees the light and tastes of the things of God, yet turns away from that true experience with the Holy Spirit, will not be able to find repentance again. To do so would be to put the Son of God back up on the cross and begin driving in the nails. A thirsty land can easily soak up the rain and become good soil for a farmer. But if the land has thorns and thistles, what use is it? None. It has to be burned.

Now friends, we're talking pretty tough here, but we don't believe that you will be the ones who get incinerated. We trust that when you read these words, they will inspire you to keep the faith and never turn your back on God. After all, you've already done so much to demonstrate the love of God to others. He won't forget that! And we believe you will avoid growing indifferent and remain diligent to the end. If so, you will be following in the footsteps of those who gained the inheritance by faith and endurance.

Take Abraham for instance. God made a promise to him that he would be blessed with an abundance of descendants.

Not only did He make a promise, He also bound Himself to the promise by oath. When people take an oath, they appeal to someone or something greater than themselves to enforce it. But since there is no one greater than God, He swore by Himself. (Now when God makes a promise and takes an oath, we have two witnesses that ensure us of the fulfillment.) Abraham had to wait a long time, but he saw that promise begin to be fulfilled, and we have seen its total spiritual fulfillment in the Messiah. Now then, God is completely trustworthy, and if He was faithful to Abraham, He will be faithful to us. The reliability of God is our hope, and it should serve as an anchor to our souls. This High Priest has taken the veil that separated us from God's presence and ripped it in half. Because He has gone before us, we, too, may now enter that Most Holy Place!

7 Now, a moment ago we quoted the Psalm that says about Jesus, "You will forever be a Priest of the same type as Melchizedek." Let's explain that. Melchizedek, a character from the book of Genesis, was the king of Salem, and a priest of the Most High God. His name means *king of justice*, and *Salem* means *peace*, so he is also the *king of peace*. There was no record given of his lineage, no father nor mother. Nor was there a record given of his birth or his death. Rather, like the Son of God, his priesthood is ongoing.

Abraham met Melchizedek just after winning a great battle. Abraham then gave him a tenth of all the spoils of the battle that he had collected. Now, how great was Melchizedek that Abraham would give him a tenth of everything he had won?!

Contrast Melchizedek's priesthood against that of the Levites. The sons of Levi who serve as priests in the Mosaic Law receive a tithe from all of the other Israelites. But the Israelites who pay these tithes (and the Israelites who collect these tithes) are all descendants of Abraham. So, Abraham is their superior in terms of order. And Abraham paid a tithe to Melchizedek, so Melchizedek is superior to Abraham. Technically, when Abraham paid his tithe to Melchizedek, all of the Levites were also paying tithes to Melchizedek, since they were "in Abraham" (that is, they were seed in Abraham's loins) at the time. This shows that Melchizedek's priesthood is greater than Levi's is. Melchizedek also blessed Abraham, and the one who gives the blessing is always greater than the one who is blessed. Not only that, the Levitical priests all lived and died, but Melchizedek lives on, proving once again that his priesthood is greater than that of the Levites.

And so we are told that Jesus is a Priest from this other type of priesthood, Melchizedek's type. Why? Why would we need Him to be of a different type? What was wrong with the priesthood of the Levites? Very simply this: the perfection of the saints that God desires could never have been made possible through that old system. But the new system that Jesus has invoked *does* perfect us to the core. And not only does the priesthood change, but the Law itself changes, because the Law says the priests must be from the tribe of Levi, but Jesus came from the tribe of Judah.

So, Jesus, a different kind of Priest, of the same type as Melchizedek, has come on the scene, being qualified for His priesthood not by virtue of Levitical lineage, but by virtue of His superior eternal life. This is what the psalmist meant when he said, "You will forever be a priest of the same type as Melchizedek." And Jesus' priesthood was established by God's oath, as it is written, "God has sworn an oath on which He will never go back: You will forever be a priest of the same type as Melchizedek."

To sum up, the old covenant was not able to achieve complete and permanent results in terms of making us righteous and making us holy. We needed a new covenant to do all of that. And indeed it does more than that, because it actually allows us to draw near to God! And Jesus is the Guarantor of this new, better covenant. He's a High Priest who is holy and undefiled and seated on high. Whereas the priests in the old system all died, preventing them from continuing in their duties, Jesus' priesthood continues forever, and He is continually interceding on behalf of those who come to God through Him. Whereas the

priests in the old system had to make sacrifices for themselves
before making sacrifices for the people, Jesus only had to
sacrifice Himself once and for all, because He was without sin.
Whereas the priests in the old system were weak, mere humans
like us, Jesus is forever perfect, and He has been appointed to be
our High Priest according to an oath taken by God Almighty.

8 Now here's the main point of everything we've said so far.
We now have a High Priest, of the Melchizedek type, who is
seated in heaven, wielding all of the power and authority of the
Father. He offers Himself in worship, thereby making our
worship acceptable, too. He ministers in the true tabernacle, not
a manmade holy place. (Remember when God gave Moses the
instructions for building the tabernacle, He told him, "Be sure
you build it according to the *pattern* I have given you on this
mountain." That Mosaic tabernacle was a mere shadow or copy
of the *pattern* that is the true tabernacle in heaven. Likewise, the
gifts and sacrifices that the priests offered in that place are mere
shadows or copies of the *pattern* that is the gift and sacrifice of
Jesus Himself.)

Jesus' ministry is not a copy of the real thing; it *is* the real
thing. As our ultimate High Priest He mediates a better covenant
for us, which is based on better promises. If the first covenant
had been sufficient, there would be no need for this new one.
But the fact is, it was insufficient. So, God promised a new one,
and He described, through Jeremiah, what that new covenant
would be like. He said:

> I'm going to make a new covenant with Israel and Judah.
> It will be different from the covenant I made with their
> ancestors when I brought them out of Egypt. (They
> were not faithful to that covenant, and I removed Myself
> from them.) This is the new covenant I will make. I'm
> going to inhabit their very hearts and minds. They won't
> have to go searching for Me, because I will be in them. I
> will be their God, and they will be My people. I will give
> them new inclinations. Whereas now they are naturally

inclined away from Me, in that day they will be naturally inclined toward Me. All they will have to do is follow their consciences, because I will be prompting those consciences to lead them down the right paths. They are going to know Me intimately. Nobody will have to teach them how to get to know Me. My mercy will cover their unrighteousness, and their sins will be forgotten.

Now since there is a new covenant, the first one is obsolete. It is fading away and will soon become a distant memory.

9 The first covenant had many rules and regulations about where and how the gifts and sacrifices were to be offered. First of all, a special tent called a tabernacle was pitched. Upon entering the tent one would find the lampstand, the table, and the sacred showbread. This first room in the tent was called the Holy Place. It was separated by a veil from the Most Holy Place, further inside the tent. In that room rested the golden altar of incense and the Ark of the Covenant. This Ark was covered in gold and contained a gold jar of manna, the staff of Aaron that budded, and the tablets of the covenant. The lid of the Ark featured cherubim with outstretched wings, which formed the mercy seat where the very presence of God sat. Every single one of these elements finds its fulfillment in Jesus, but we don't have time right now to explain all that.

Now, the priests regularly went into the first part of the tabernacle to perform their duties, but the High Priest alone entered the Most Holy Place, and only once a year. And when he did so, he offered blood for his own sins and for the sins of the people he represented. The Holy Spirit was showing us by these restrictive rules that the Most Holy Place was not a place of open access as long as the tabernacle system was in operation. Similarly, the gifts and sacrifices only made the people ceremonially clean, they did not result in open access to the presence of God where their consciences could be washed clean.

But now that the Messiah has become our High Priest, ministering in the better tabernacle that is not of this world, having entered the Most Holy Place once for all, not by the blood of bulls and goats, but by His own blood, we can expect better things: open access to God, eternal redemption, cleansed consciences. For if the blood of bulls and goats was capable of purifying the body, how much more will the blood of Jesus be capable? Yes, to purify us to our very core so that we can serve God joyfully from a place of freedom, and not nervously from a place of obligation.

Now it was by His death that He became the Mediator of this New Covenant, solving all of the problems of sin that remained under the first covenant. And it was by His death that He secured our inheritance. For the collecting of an inheritance is always contingent on the death of the one leaving the inheritance. Even the first covenant was enacted with blood. You may remember that Moses sprinkled the blood of calves and goats on the book of the Law and on the people, on the tabernacle itself and on the vessels of ministry, proclaiming, "This blood puts God's covenant with you into effect." Nearly everything in the Law is purified by blood, because without blood there is no forgiveness.

The copies of the heavenly pattern had to be purified by animal blood, but the pattern itself—the tabernacle of heaven and all that it entails—are pure by virtue of Christ's blood. And now He has entered heaven to appear before God on our behalf. He did not have to offer Himself over and over, as the sacrifices of the first system were offered. His death and resurrection was a one-time event that was effectual for all people for all time. Everyone has an appointed time to die, and afterward to receive judgment. But Jesus died to beat the sin problem once and for all, that we may avoid the judgment of the second death. To those who eagerly await Him, He will return again, not to deliver us from sin, but to bring our salvation to its completion.

10 Once again, the Law, as a mere shadow of the good things to come, did not and could not ever perfect the one offering the sacrifice. Those sacrifices were offered year after year, proving that they were insufficient. Why would they need to be offered the second year if the first year was sufficient? No, in offering the sacrifices, the people were actually reminded of their sin and their continual position of unrighteousness. But in the new system, those who have faith in Christ's one sacrifice are cleansed perpetually, and even our consciences are clean. He no longer remembers our sin, and we don't have to either.

Jesus confirmed this changeover of the covenants by His own word. First He said, "God, you really have no need or desire for burnt offerings and sacrifices." And second He said, "I have come to do Your will, God." (And God's will was that we would be made holy through Jesus' sacrifice.) Now the first statement nullifies the first covenant, and the second statement establishes the new covenant.

So, Jesus sacrificed Himself, once for all (not like the repetitive sacrifices of the Levitical priests), then He assumed the authority of His kingship, sitting upon His heavenly throne, waiting for the day when His enemies will be placed under His feet. He has forgiven us, He has perfected those who are being made holy, and He has written His laws on our minds and put them into our hearts. The Holy Spirit is a witness to us of all these things, saying, "I'll put My laws in their hearts, and write them on their minds. I won't remember their sins anymore." Now, since all of this has been accomplished, there is no need for any more sacrifices.

Therefore, brothers and sisters, let's boldly enter that Most Holy Place with strong faith in our High Priest, drawing near to God, through the entrance that Jesus made possible by His death, having our consciences washed by His blood and our bodies washed with pure water. Let's hold on to our hope, and not turn back from the faith. The God who gave us the promise will be faithful to keep it. Let's stir each other up to grow in love and continually do good. Let's not stop meeting together (as some have done), but keep on encouraging each other, and all the more so as that final Day gets closer.

For if we go back to our old sinful ways after having come

into the knowledge of Jesus by the illumination of the Holy Spirit, there will no longer be a sacrifice to cover that sin. No, those who turn back will be met with a judgment of fire doled out by a zealous God. Count on it! Anyone who rebels against Moses' Law is executed on the testimony of two or three witnesses. There's no mercy there. Don't you know how much worse it will be for those who have spurned the Son of God, treated the blood that made them holy as though it were a common thing, and insulted the Holy Spirit who is rich in grace? God Himself has said, "Revenge belongs to Me. I will repay," and "I will judge My people." It is *terrifying* to fall into the hands of the Living God!

Remember back to the time when you first came into the faith, and you were persecuted for it. Some of you endured ridicule, some endured beatings, some were imprisoned, some endured the confiscation of all your possessions, and you encouraged those who endured the same. You endured all of these things because you recognized that something better was waiting just around the corner, not only better, but also eternal.

So don't lay aside your unreserved fearlessness; it will result in a great reward. What you need is endurance, so that you can persevere until the time that your salvation is completed. Remember, the Son is the *Sustainer of all things*. He has done everything needed to get you across the finish line. Continue on in God's will and you will receive the fulfillment of the promise. Be cautioned and encouraged by Habakkuk's words: "He will be coming very soon! And those who keep the faith will be found righteous when He comes, but He will find no pleasure with those who turn away." But we aren't going to be the ones who turn away, right?! We are the ones who will continue on in faith until our salvation is completed.

11 Now faith is the revealed reality of the things that we expect with confident assurance, and the proof of the things we "Spir"-ceive (that is to say, the things we "catch by the Spirit"). It was by faith that the ancient saints developed a certain amount of spiritual prestige. It is by faith that we understand that God created the universe, and everything that we can see originated in One who cannot be seen.

It was because of faith that Abel's offering was deemed acceptable, whereas it was the lack of faith that made Cain's offering unacceptable. It was because of faith that God spared Enoch from death by taking him off of the earth to be with Him. And it was said of Enoch that he *pleased* God. Well, it takes faith to please God. We must not only believe that God exists, but also believe that He rewards everyone who diligently seeks Him. It was by faith that Noah built the Ark in order to save his family (and the animals God entrusted to him) from a flood that nobody else believed was coming. But Noah believed because he heard God speak.

It was by faith that Abraham obtained his promise. He, too, obeyed the voice of God, which told him to go to the place he would receive an inheritance. And he went out, not even knowing where he was going. He lived in the land of promise— He and his two heirs of the promise, Isaac and Jacob—even though the promise had not yet fully been fulfilled. And he waited for the fulfillment, never losing faith in the process. It was by faith that Sarah obtained her promise, too. She was well past the age to have children, and yet she believed God could do what He said. And from these two came the innumerable descendants that were promised.

Now even though none of these folks ever saw the total fulfillment of God's promise to mankind—that is, Jesus—they all nevertheless continued on in the faith for as long as they remained on earth. They all understood that the world was a temporary residence, and they all looked forward to a new home. It's because of this faith that God is not ashamed to be called their God. And the home that they looked forward to, He has prepared for them.

It was by faith that Abraham passed his test when God asked him to offer up Isaac, even though God had already promised Abraham descendants through Isaac. Abraham believed that even if he had to go through with the sacrifice,

God was willing and able to raise Isaac from the dead. That's how sure Abraham was that the Word of the Lord is trustworthy. After that, it was Isaac who blessed Jacob and Esau by faith. Then Jacob blessed the sons of Joseph by faith, as he leaned on his staff and worshipped. Then Joseph prophesied the Exodus of the Israelites by faith, even though that would not happen for another 400 years, and he gave instructions on what to do with his bones.

It was by faith that Moses' parents hid him for three months, without giving in to any fears they may have had regarding the king and his command. It was by faith that Moses later associated himself with the lowly Hebrews instead of claiming the good life of the palace and the temporary pleasures of sin that came with it. Even he was suffering "for Christ's sake" in making that choice. It was by faith that Moses left Egypt for Midian with his eyes stayed on the invisible God, not on the powerful Egyptian king. It was by faith that he returned to Egypt, stood up to Pharaoh, commanded the people in regards to the Passover, and led the people out of Egypt by way of the miraculous Red Sea crossing.

It was by faith that the walls of Jericho fell. They couldn't stand under the weight of seven days of obedience. Meanwhile it was by faith that Rahab the prostitute was saved, because of her act of kindness toward the spies.

On and on it goes. We don't have time now to keep giving example after example of those who have come before us who have lived by faith. But the examples are there. People like Gideon, Barak, Samson, Jephthah, David, Samuel, and the Prophets, who toppled kingdoms, ruled with justice, obtained promises, shut up lion's mouths, quenched the raging fire, escaped the edge of the sword, found strength through weakness, became mighty warriors and forced their enemies into full retreat. The dead were raised to life and were returned to the women who loved them. But others were tortured for their faith, without ever giving in, knowing that it would all be worth it in the end. Others were mocked, others whipped, others imprisoned, others stoned, others sawed in two, others chopped down by sword, others were left destitute and afflicted, traversing deserts and hiding in caves. Yet none of these people received the final fulfillment of the promise. God was holding on to something better, which we get to receive. And now, they are being made perfect, along with us.

12 Now since we have such a large company of examples to encourage us, let's be sure to run our race well, enduring to the end. The only way to make it is to continually focus on Jesus, who is not only the author of our faith, but also the One who brings it to completion. If He could endure the cross, we also should endure whatever persecution comes to us. If He was able to rise above the shame of that terrible circumstance, so should we be able to rise above any embarrassment we may face. If He was able to keep His mind set on the joy that He knew was on the other side, so should we. He went all the way, giving His very life. We haven't done that yet.

Did you forget that God has spoken to us as His children? He said, "My child, don't despise my discipline. Don't get discouraged when I correct you. If you're receiving My discipline, it means I love you. And when I give you a spanking, it's a sign to you that you're Mine." See, receiving God's discipline proves you belong to Him. If He doesn't correct you, you're illegitimate. Even earthly fathers discipline and correct their children, and we respect them for it. How much more should we respect God when He corrects us? Our earthly fathers didn't always get it right when they disciplined us. But God always gets it right, because He's perfect and He loves us perfectly, and His purpose in that discipline is that we would become holy! Of course, nobody enjoys discipline and correction. It hurts. But later, after its seeds have been cultivated, the fruit of righteousness and holiness it produces proves the worth of the process. So, get ahold of yourselves, and continue moving forward.

Make it a top priority to maintain peace with everyone, as well as holiness. If you're not holy, you won't make it to heaven.

Period. Be on guard. Don't fail to actually seize God's grace. Don't let any feelings of bitterness take root and begin to pollute your spirit. Don't be like Esau and trade a holy life for a careless and common life. He was never able to get back what he lost, even though he was sorry for the choices he made. If you're not pursuing holiness, you're pursuing immorality.

The New Covenant is a spiritual thing, not a physical thing, so the seriousness of it can escape us if we're not careful to keep it before our spiritual eyes. When the Israelites came to Mount Sinai, there was a tangible holiness to that place such that they even heard God say, "Anyone who touches this mountain must be stoned, even animals." They were petrified at the darkness and fire and fierce wind. Even Moses admitted he was shaking in terror. But we're not at Mount Sinai, we're at Mount Zion, the city of God where angels worship and God judges and Jesus mediates a better covenant by His blood. Oh, Church! Don't refuse to listen to His commands. If the Israelites didn't escape when they refused to listen to Moses, we won't escape if we refuse to listen to Jesus. He said, "I'm going to shake heaven and earth one last time," which tells us that only what's unshakable will remain after that. So, since we are inheriting an unshakable kingdom, let's make sure we fully tap into the grace of God in order to be empowered to serve God acceptably, with fear and reverence, because our God is a fire that incinerates every trace of unholiness in its path.

13 Love each other well. Show hospitality even to strangers, because you may actually be entertaining angels without even realizing it. It's happened before. Remember those who have been imprisoned for the faith, as if it were you yourself. Keep your marriages honorable before God and the world; we know that God will judge all adulterers and fornicators. Don't be jealous of others, but be content with whatever you have. After all, we have Him, and He's all we need! He has promised that He would never leave us and never give up on us. So boldly proclaim, "The Lord is my helper. I won't be afraid of anybody."

Obey your spiritual leaders. They're looking out for you, and they're accountable for you. So make their lives and yours a bit easier by submitting. Imitate these spiritual mentors who have taught you God's Word and proven themselves by their conduct.

Jesus Christ is the same, yesterday, today, and forever. So don't let yourself get reeled in by a bunch of newfangled doctrines. Rules about what kinds of foods you should eat, and other similar nonsense, are additions to the true faith that simply do not have the eternal effectiveness that grace-alone does. We have an altar from which those of the Mosaic covenant can't eat. They took the bodies of the sacrificed animals outside the camp and burned them. But we have Jesus, who suffered and died outside the city walls. Let's not be ashamed or afraid to embrace the disapproval that the world showed Him.

Our earthly homes will not continue on indefinitely; only the eternal home that we are looking forward to does that. So let's continually praise God with a sacrificial praise. (And giving to those in need is what constitutes a pleasing sacrifice.)

Okay, I think that's all for now. Please go back and reread this letter, and pay close attention to everything I have said here. Grace be with you all. Amen.

Please pray for us. Our consciences are clean. We are doing everything we know to do to live holy and honorable before God. Pray especially that we can come see you soon. Speaking of which, Timothy has been released from prison. If he is able to join up with me, I'll plan on bringing him with me to see you. Please say "Hi" to everyone there for me. Everybody in Italy sends their greetings as well.

Now may the God of peace, who raised from the dead our Great Shepherd and Lord, Jesus, complete the work of making you exactly who and what He wants you to be, through the blood of His eternal covenant. To Him be all glory forever and ever. Amen.

Discussion Questions

WEEK 1: Hebrews 1-7

- Why was it necessary that our substitutionary sacrifice be fully human *and* fully divine?
- What is the nature and purpose of the comparison given in Chapter 3 between Jesus and Moses?
- Explain the difference between the two priesthoods (Melchizedek's and Levi's/Aaron's). How does Jesus fit into this whole priest history?
- Three strong warnings are interpolated throughout Hebrews 1-7. Discuss these warnings. In particular, consider how serious they are given the context of the passages around them.

WEEK 2: Hebrews 8-13

- The New Covenant is described as being written "on our hearts" and "in our minds." What does this mean and how is it different from the Old Covenant? Do God's laws and ways saturate *your* heart and mind?
- In Hebrews 10 we learn that those who first received this letter had already been persecuted for their faith. Talk about how much more seriously we should observe the warnings in the letter given this fact.
- Why was the "Hall of Faith" (Chapter 11) included in this letter?
- Chapters 12-13 give the practical application of the letter. What jumped out at you in this section about how the Christian life should be lived?

THE LETTERS TO THE CHURCH FROM

JOHN

1 My dear little children in the faith,

I'm writing to encourage you. I want you to grab hold of this truth we've been proclaiming, so that it may cause you to overflow with joy. The message that we delivered to you, the message that I'm reiterating now, is 100% trustworthy. It's not like we just overheard some random story. No, we were there! We saw His miracles, we heard Him speak directly to us for over three years, and we touched the wounds in His hands after His resurrection. This Man was, absolutely, without doubt, the Word of God and the Life of God, made incarnate. We have given a firsthand account full of eyewitness testimony. And we want you to believe in this testimony, so that you, like us, will be able to maintain fellowship with the Father, and with the Son, who is Jesus, the Christ.

Now, this is the message: *God is light, and there's not a hint of darkness in Him at all.* If you claim that you are "saved" and maintaining a right relationship with God, and yet you are still walking in the darkness of sin, you're a liar, plain and simple. But if you allow the light of God to illuminate every dark place in your heart, and you give over to Him every idolatrous thought and action that His light exposes, then you are cleansed by Jesus' blood, and we can truly call you our brothers and sisters.

Anyone who would be so arrogant as to claim that he is righteous on his own merit is totally deceived and does not possess the truth. Everybody has sinned, and anyone who says otherwise blasphemously implies that God is a liar. But if we confess our sins in a true posture of repentance, He will forgive us and wash us clean from any and all unrighteousness.

2 I'm writing all of this with the assumption that it will inspire you to live a sin-free life, but if it so happens that someone does sin, Jesus Himself serves continually as our Defense Attorney before the Father. Because He is the propitiation, that is to say *covering*, for our sins (actually, for the sins of the whole world), He can simply stress to the Father that His death substituted for ours, our punishment was transferred onto Him, and our true legal verdict is *not guilty*.

Can I just make it really simple? Here's how you can know that you're in fellowship with God: *by doing everything He says to do.* If you claim to know God, and yet you don't do what He says to do, you're a liar. You have chosen to ignore the truth. If you obey Him, He will complete His work of filling you up with His love. If you are truly abiding in Him, the way you live your life will look like the way Jesus lived His.

Children, I'm not telling you anything you don't already know. Technically, this is Judaism 101. And yet, it is somehow new, too, because the Holy Spirit has breathed new life into this old commandment. We have to understand that possessing and demonstrating the love of God is central to the Christian life.

The Light has come into the world, and the darkness has begun to fade away. Anyone who claims to be in the light, yet hates a fellow Christian, is actually in darkness. And in that darkness, you can't see where you're going because you're blind. But those who love one another walk in the light, and they can see clearly where they're going.

Church, be encouraged today if you are among those who walk in the light. I'm telling you all: you know the Father, and your sins are forgiven through Jesus! Mature saints, hear me: you know Christ, the eternal One! Young people, the battle against the enemy of your soul has already been won! God's word lives in you, and you are strong!

Don't let your hearts pine after the world and its things. And don't love the world's ways and the world's systems and the world's pleasures and the world's values. Anyone who loves these things has no clue about the Father's love.

All sin falls into three categories: the unholy desire for what feels good, the unholy desire for what looks good, and the pride in what we have and what we've done. All three categories of sin are worldly, not from the Father. For people who give in to their unholy desires, what the world offers them is disintegrating, but people who let God fulfill all their desires will live forever.

When I say that the world as we know it is dying and will soon be no more, what I mean is, the end times have commenced. You've heard people talk about how the Antichrist will come? Well, here's how we know that we're now living in the beginning of the end times: many antichrists have already come. What is *antichrist*? It's anything that is "against Jesus." Any teaching that is even a single degree out of alignment with spiritual true-north is of the spirit of antichrist. And anyone who perpetrates such a teaching is an antichrist. An antichrist denies that Jesus is the Messiah, the Son of God who came to save the world. By denying the Son, they also deny the Father, because you can't accept one without accepting both. Now, we've seen these antichrists come and go. They were part of our fellowship, posing as believers. But time and circumstance eventually revealed who they really were, and they have abandoned the fellowship, proving that they are not actually of God. You're not like them though. You have been anointed by the Holy Spirit to be able to discern between truth and lies. His anointing will remain on you—if you continue on in Him—to show you what is real and what is counterfeit. Be careful to make sure that the pure truth you believed at the start remains in you. For the reward promised us for remaining in Him is eternal life. So remain in the Son and in the Father, and you will not be ashamed when He appears. For God is righteous, and you will show that you are born of Him if you act righteously.

3 Think about the magnificent greatness of God's love toward us. He even calls us His children! The world doesn't understand that because they don't know Him. Even we don't understand what we are going to become when He is fully revealed to us and we see Him as He actually is, but we do know that we will be like Him. And those who look forward to this seek to become more and more pure.

Again, let's not complicate the issue. Anyone who lives in sin is of the devil, who has been sinning since the beginning. And the person who sins is breaking God's law. If you're abiding in Jesus, you will not continue in sin. Jesus is sinless, and He came to liberate us from sin and to render the devil impotent in everything he attempts. So there's no excuse for continuing in sin, and if you do continue in it, you're proving you're not God's, you've never seen Him, and you've never known Him. The one who practices righteousness is righteous, but the one who hates his brother and doesn't do right is not of God. Don't let anyone tell you differently.

This is the message you have heard from the beginning: love each other. Loving the Christian brothers and sisters is a sign that you have passed from death to life. If instead you hate somebody in the Family, you're just like Cain. He murdered his brother out of jealousy for his acceptable offering, knowing that his own offering was not acceptable. Those who hate God's children in this way are murderers in their hearts even if they never follow through with the action. And you know that no murderer can inherit eternal life. On the other hand, if you are following the Lord in purity and living acceptably before Him, don't be surprised if people hate you for it.

Well, what does it look like to love each other? Jesus demonstrated it. He laid down His very life for us. That's the level of commitment we should have for each other. For example, if you who are well-off see a brother or sister in need, yet you are not willing to meet that need, how can you say the love of God resides in you? God's love is not merely lip service. It bears out in actions.

How do we know if we're right with God and walking according to His Truth? We know by His Holy Spirit who lives in us. The Spirit will arrest you when you get out of line, and if you will listen and adjust every time you feel His correction, you can live life with a clean conscience, knowing you are pleasing to Him. If you feel guilty about something, repent and turn it over to God, trusting Him to wipe the slate clean. Then you can continue on in the practice of obeying His command. If we boil it down, His command is to trust in Jesus to empower you to live a life that is pleasing to Him, which includes loving each other. Once you get to the place where you know in your heart of hearts that you are doing everything you know to do to be pleasing to Him, you can be confident that you will receive anything you ask of Him!

4 Not every spirit within our ranks is of God. You need to examine the things people say and do, to discern whether the spirit behind those things is from God. How do we know? Well, for one thing, anybody who claims that Jesus was not a real flesh-and-bone human being is not speaking by the Spirit of God, but rather speaks by the spirit of Antichrist. Don't even think about listening to anybody's teaching if they do not affirm the truth that Jesus is both 100% God and 100% man. Such people are worldly, and when they speak what the world wants to hear, the world listens. But God's not listening. He only listens to you, those who are His. The Spirit of God living in you is greater than the spirit they're operating in. That's why our testimony will outlast theirs. If you are God's children, you will hear with your spiritual ears those things that are from His Spirit, and He will help you to distinguish truth from error.

Dear Church, I tell you again: love one another. There is a God-kind-of-love that you can only receive and express to others if you're born of God and know God. Those who don't practice that kind of love don't know God, because that love is an essential and inseparable facet of His God-ness. Now, this is the way in which God made His kind of love a tangible reality: He sent His Son to die in our place so that we could be set free from sin and join Him in His eternal, effervescent mode of living. If the way He expressed His love was through sacrificial giving, that should be the way we express love, too.

Nobody has actually seen God, but when we are loving toward one another, we know that He is living in us and His love has been accomplished within us. And that completed work of love in us will give us the confidence to stand before Him on Judgment Day, because if we live our lives here on earth the way Jesus lived His, we have nothing to worry about. God's love shatters all fear. If you're just trying to live a "good life" because you're fearful of the punishment you'll receive if you don't, then you haven't really received the full revelation of His love yet. God expressed His love toward us by sending His Son to save the world, so it is imperative that one believe in the Son in order to receive the impartation of God's love by His Spirit. When we stay connected to God, His love flows back and forth between us and Him, and then out from us to others.

We love God because God loved us first. You can't claim to love God and yet hate your brother; that's not following His commandment. How can you love the God you haven't seen if you can't even love the brother that you do see?

5 You must believe that Jesus is the Christ—King over Israel, King over the whole earth, and King over you personally—in order to be born again. Everyone who truly loves the Father loves the Son, also. I know I keep driving this point home, but let me say it one last time: you must receive the Son in order to receive the Father, you must obey Him, and you must love one another, because that's the evidence that you love God. When we keep the commandment of God in this way, it's not a burden. In fact, it is our faith in Father God and in His Son that assures us of victory over the world.

What testimony do we have that Jesus is the Son of God and the only way to the eternal life found in the Father? God's own personal testimony! Remember it was Father God who testified that Jesus was His own Son when He was baptized in the Jordan. The Spirit of God testified as well, descending as a dove and remaining on Him. Then Jesus Himself testified that He was the Christ by pouring out His own blood for our sakes, being resurrected to new life by God's power. So, you see, we have three witnesses: the witness of the Holy Spirit who anointed Him, the witness of the Father who claimed Him, and the witness of the Son who died for us. Anyone who believes in the Son of God has that witness within himself. Anyone who doesn't believe in the Son has rejected God's own testimony and has made Him out to be a liar. Whoever receives God's Son has life, and whoever doesn't receive Him doesn't have life.

Children, I have written these things to you who believe in the Son so that you can be assured that you have eternal life, also so that you will continue to believe. And here is the confidence we have if we believe: everything we ask of Him that aligns with His will, He hears, and we, in turn, know we have whatever we ask for. So pray for the saints when you see them enter into sin. Those prayers will be answered, guaranteed. (Now, we're not talking about the very grievous sins. We all know that anyone who turns away from the truth in order to practice the filthy, vile behaviors of the world, is headed for death. Don't even bother praying against that kind of apostate rebellion. But there is a kind of sin that does not lead to death. A kind of sin that God corrects in stride as part of the sanctification process. If you see brothers or sisters entering into those kinds of sins, pray for them that God will correct them and they will turn and continue on in His perfect will.) We know that anyone born of God does not keep on sinning. The Son protects all of God's children, and the enemy has no access to them. The entire rest of the world is directed by the enemy, but we are directed by God. We know that the Son of God has come and enlightened us, showing us who He is, the Truth and the Eternal Life. And we are in Him, in that Truth, in that Life. So, dear little children, you have but one job to do: don't let anyone or anything usurp the throne of your heart, for it is reserved for God alone. Oh, God, let it be so.

Your loving father in the faith,
John

To the Church and Her members, chosen by God,

I declare to you that grace, peace, and mercy from God the Father and from His Son Jesus Christ will be with you as you walk in truth and allow His love to take root in you. I have a truly authentic love for you—not only I, but everyone who walks according to the truth. And I am very excited to hear that some of you are walking according to the truth, too.

Now, I'm writing to you in order to impress upon you strongly the need to love one another. This is not a new commandment, but God is reminding us of it with a new fervor. We show that we love Him by loving others. You'll remember Jesus said this two-part commandment was the greatest. We must walk according to His commandment.

Heed this warning, Church. A bunch of folks are going around claiming that Jesus did not actually come to earth as a flesh-and-bone human being. Anyone who says such things is speaking by the spirit of Antichrist, and is not of God. They are trying to deceive you. Don't let them! Stay on guard, and don't lose the truth that you have received. That's the only way to hold on to the reward. Anyone who rejects the full humanity *and* full divinity of Christ does not have God. But you who believe in the Son have access to the Father also. They're a package-deal. You cannot receive the Father without receiving the Son. If anyone preaches any message contrary to this, don't receive him into your house, neither speak blessing over him. If you do, you will be partaking in evil by aligning yourself with evil.

I have much more to say, but I'm going to save the paper and ink for now because I'm hoping to get to come see you and talk to you face to face. That will be wonderful! For now, we'll say "goodbye." Everybody from the church here sends greetings.

Your loving elder,
John

Discussion Questions

WEEK 3: 1 John & 2 John

- The opening two paragraphs of John's first epistle give the author's credentials, his purpose for writing, and his overarching message. Articulate each in your own words.

- One of the major themes of 1 John is *love*. How does John's discussion of love compare/contrast with some of your own assumptions of what love looks like?

- The other major theme in 1 John is *antichrist*. How does John's discussion of the spirit of Antichrist differ with any pictures you may have about an end-times character who goes by the same name?

- How would you say the message of 2 John compares to that of 1 John?

THE LETTER FROM

JAMES

1 Greetings to all of the Jewish believers who are scattered all over the known world,

I have several things on my heart to share with you. I can say with confidence that what I am writing to you today is directly from the Lord and extremely important, so please take note.

First, you need to have the perspective that when difficult trials come your way, they provide you with an opportunity to grow in the Lord. That should be an occasion for joy! Some of the fruit that the Holy Spirit produces in you can only ripen as you endure hard times. When you allow your faith to be tested by difficult circumstances, patience comes forth in you, and patience leads to a completeness. See, we want to get to the point where we lack no good thing from God. Now, if you do feel yourself running low on, say, wisdom, for instance, just petition the Lord for it. He will not balk at sharing His nature with you. Of course, you have to ask Him in faith, without doubting, believing that it will be done, otherwise you shouldn't expect to receive anything from the Lord. The one who tries to have faith while also entertaining doubts is double-minded and unstable, like a wave of a sea that gets driven about by external forces. We are to be people who are driven solely by the One who is within us.

So, those who are poor: boast in God for a trial that is exalting you higher in Him. And those who are rich: boast in God for every circumstance that humbles you, because in the end, all of your riches will be wiped away, and the only thing you'll have left is whatever character was developed in you during the tough circumstances. Just like the grass turns brown and the beautiful flower diminishes to nothing, so the rich and all of their accomplishments will fade away.

Resisting temptation leads to happiness. There is a proving that takes place in that moment. And at the end of our proving process, having been found faithful, we will receive from God the crown of life. Don't blame temptations on God. He's not in that business. No, we are tempted by our own desires, the weaknesses we have left exposed to the enemy. When you don't curb your unholy desires, you initiate a disturbing life-cycle, an ugly creature that is conceived as a carnal appetite and birthed as sin; and if that sin is not eradicated, it ends in death. None of that is from God, of course, so don't be deceived into thinking it might be. On the contrary, God is in the business of giving good gifts. Nothing good can come from any source other than Him. Furthermore, He is consistent in His goodness. You don't have to worry about Him being good toward you one minute and hating you the next. After all, He birthed you, you are His child, He has implanted His truth in you, and you hold the favored position among everything He created.

So, be careful to do what's right at every turn. Be quick to listen and slow to speak. Anyone who thinks he is on the straight-and-narrow, yet has no control over his tongue, is deceived. Pure and undefiled religion consists of keeping yourself holy and loving those who are down and out. So don't allow a single speck of the world's filth to taint you, and be helpful and generous to the widows and orphans.

Also, don't let yourself get angry easily. Man's anger is not compatible with God's righteousness. You've got to put away all of the evil ways you used to walk in, and with a mild disposition allow God's Holy Word to take root in you and grow until it bears fruit. That's the only way your soul can be saved.

You can't just hear the Word preached or read the Word on a page, and not then go put that Word into action. That would be like looking at yourself in the mirror and then walking away and forgetting what you look like. That's not the purpose of a mirror, and that's not the purpose of the Word. On the other hand, if you study God's ways and God's principles intently and honestly, being sure to put them into practice, you will be happy in everything you do.

2 Church, don't allow people's physical appearance to be a determining factor in the way you treat them. Let's say two different men come into your gathering, one rich and well dressed, one poor and disheveled. You can't show honor to the one and ignore the other. To do that would be to make a judgment from evil motives. Don't you remember what Jesus said about the rich and the poor? The poor have a special place in God's economy, and they are much more likely to inherit the kingdom than the rich are. I mean, think about some of the rich people you know. They have a reputation of un-Christlike behavior, do they not? Exerting power and control over you, taking you to court, blaspheming God's Name? The command to "Love your neighbor as yourself" applies to everyone. Showing favoritism is sin. Does it matter what sin you engage in? It's all sin. The Law says, "Don't murder," and it also says, "Don't commit adultery." If you commit adultery, you can't just appeal to the fact you haven't committed murder. No, if you break one of the laws, you're guilty of breaking them all. So, don't show favoritism. It's a transgression just like any other. You would be wise to remember that you're going to be judged one day by a God who has mercifully set us free, but you will not receive that mercy if you have not shown mercy to others. So, when you're in position to judge, err on the side of showing mercy.

Here's something else to consider. What's the point of saying you have faith if you have no actions to prove it? Can you really be saved through that kind of "faith"? If you see a Christian brother or sister living in destitution, and you just speak a little blessing over them instead of actually meeting their needs, what good does that do? The kind of faith that produces no actions is worthless. Don't give me some bogus line about certain people having faith and other people having actions. Malarkey! Anyone who has faith will be able to prove it with faith-based actions. Are you really going to defend yourself by touting your good theology? You know the demons believe all the same things you do, right? And their "faith" even makes them tremble in fear. It doesn't really help them in the end though, does it? You fool! Faith without actions is dead!

Wasn't our father Abraham deemed righteous on account of his actions? He was willing to go all the way in sacrificing Isaac. And the Scripture says that Abraham *believed* and so was counted righteous and was called God's friend. That's such a clear picture of faith and actions working in tandem. So, you see, a man is justified by actions, not by faith alone.

Then there was Rahab. Didn't she also attain righteousness by her faith-based action when she put the spies up and then sent them out another way? Yes, just as the body without the spirit is dead, so faith without actions is dead.

3 Church, don't let many members become teachers. Understand that teachers will be judged according to a higher standard.

We all miss the mark sometimes, but the one who is able to keep from missing the mark in what he says is truly in control of himself. Just like a bit in a horse's mouth that allows the whole animal to be turned, or a little rudder that steers a huge ship, so the tongue is the instrument that commands the fate of the whole body.

Likewise, a tiny spark can cause a devastating forest fire. And the tongue *is* a fire, speaking all the selfishness that lies in the heart. It props itself up as the leader among the body parts, and then leads the body right to the fire of hell itself. Somebody who knows what he's doing can tame about any kind of animal you can think of, yet nobody can seem to tame his own tongue. It's unruly, evil, and full of deadly poison. One minute it's praising God, and the next minute it's cursing the very people that God made in His image. It is totally illogical to think that blessing and cursing could come from the same mouth. Can you draw both fresh water and salt water from the same spring? Not any more than you can pick a fig off a grapevine or a grape off a fig tree.

Who among you is learned and scholarly? Let him prove his credentials by living a good life in the humility that comes from gaining more and more knowledge. If you have jealousy and selfish ambition in your heart, don't be fake and try to make people think you don't. Come clean with those impure motives, and humble yourself until the Lord scrubs that stain out of the fabric of your life. The jealous and ambitious operate according to ungodly, demonic impulses. Where there is jealousy and selfish ambition, every other form of evil also exists. But God's wisdom is pure, peace-loving, gentle, compliant, merciful, fruitful, fair, and sincere. And he who sows in peace reaps in righteousness.

4 What causes disputes and quarrels among you? The evil desires wreaking havoc within you. You let your cravings increase, yet they are never satisfied. You even kill for what you want (spiritually speaking), yet it's still out of reach. You fight for your selfish aspirations, yet never feel accomplished. You don't have what you're going after because you don't even know what it is you should be asking for. When you do ask for something, you don't receive it, because God knows you're not going to steward it well. You're just going to funnel it back to your self-absorbed life. Stop playing the role of the cheating spouse! Don't you know that making friends with the world is an act of hostility toward God? Anyone who is a friend of the world is an enemy of God. The Scripture says, "The Spirit of God within us has intense jealously." Do you think that verse was just included arbitrarily?

It doesn't have to be that way, Church. He has an abundant supply of grace, and there's always as much as you need to be able to overcome. The key is found in this Scripture: "God resists the proud, but gives grace to the humble." So humble yourselves and submit fully to God. Stop approaching life flippantly, and begin to contemplate the gravity of your situation with sobriety. Let your sin grieve you. Cry out to Him in anguish until you receive the breakthrough and assurance of a changed heart. Keep moving closer and closer to God, and you'll see that He will keep moving closer and closer to you. Let Him purify your hearts, and let that overflow into purified actions. As you submit to God, you will be able to resist the devil. The more you allow God to change you, the more the devil will leave you alone. If you do all this, God will lift you up.

Don't bad-mouth each other, and don't pass judgment on each other. That's just the same as bad-mouthing and passing judgment on God's own law. And if you judge the law, you're not really keeping it. There's only One who makes the law and enforces the law, and it's not you! He can save, and He can destroy. You don't have the power or authority to do either.

Don't be so foolish as to make your own plans and presume to follow through on them. You don't have the foggiest idea what's going to happen tomorrow. Hold your plans loosely, and be ready to move with the wind of the Spirit if it becomes clear that God wills something contrary to the course you've set. It's evil to go through life functioning as your own counselor, never putting up an antenna to discern God's direction. And to refuse to follow where He leads is sin.

5 You who are rich, who have gained your riches by greed and unjust treatment of others, get ready to receive your judgment. You would be weeping if you understood the misery and agony that's in store for you. Your money has already lost its value, and your fancy clothes have already been destroyed by moths; you just can't see it yet. The corrosion on your gold and silver is a testimony against you, and will destroy you in the end. The "treasure" you have accumulated for yourself amounts to an endless stream of tears. You have condemned and executed those who did nothing to deserve it. The cries of those you have mistreated have been heard by the Lord. You have given yourself to pleasure and luxury. You have fattened yourself right up for the slaughter.

So, to those who live righteously, be patient. The Lord sees everything, and He will establish justice at the appointed time.

The farmer waits patiently for the harvest, enduring the rains. In the same way wait patiently and encourage yourselves, for the Lord is coming again soon.

We have so many examples of patience and endurance in the Old Testament. Consider Job, for instance. He endured a hardship ordained by God and received a bountiful blessing on the other side, a testament to God's mercy. We have always held up patience and endurance, and the people who exhibit these qualities, as admirable and exemplary. So don't murmur against each other, Church, or else you will bring condemnation on yourselves. (Remember, the Judge is always within earshot.) More importantly, don't dare adopt the mindset that you only need to operate in integrity when you swear some kind of oath. Be a man of your word, be a woman of your word, every day and in every situation.

If anyone is enduring a hardship, that person should pray. If anyone is in good spirits, she should sing praises. If anyone is sick, he should call for the elders of the church so that they can come and pray over him, anointing him with oil in the name of the Lord. If their prayers are offered in faith, the one who is sick will be healed and raised up. If the sickness came about as a result of some sin he committed, his confession and repentance through faith will bring forgiveness. So, confess your sins to each other. If anyone has veered from the truth, make an attempt to turn him back to it; you'll literally be saving his soul from death if you're successful. And pray fervently that you may be healed. A righteous person who prays fervently is extremely effective. (Think about Elijah, who was a man just like us. He prayed fervently that God would withhold rain from the land, and there was no rain for 3½ years. Then when he prayed for the rain to resume, it resumed, and the land produced its crops.)

Well, friends, I'm going to need to bring it to a close for now. Blessings and peace to you in Jesus' name.

Your devoted servant-leader,
James, a slave of God and of the Lord Jesus Christ

Discussion Questions

WEEK 4: James

- James has quite a bit to say about rich people and poor people? Is God predisposed to be against rich people and favorable toward poor people? What sorts of things should a rich person be concerned about?

- Another major theme in this letter is the need to be careful what we say. Can you think of an example of when someone's words caused unnecessary pain? Have you fully forgiven that person? Do you need to repent of any patterns in your own speech?

- Self-centeredness seems to underpin all of the problems James addresses. Explain.

- Amid a preponderance of correction and admonition in this letter lie some beautiful promises. Identify them and discuss them.

PAUL'S LETTER TO THE
ROMANS

1 To the holy people of God living in Rome,

This is Paul. Most of you know me by reputation at least, but it's important that you recognize who is writing you. First and foremost I am a slave of Jesus Christ. I'm also an apostle, called to preach the Gospel. "What's the Gospel?" you ask. It is the good news that Jesus, who not only comes from the royal line of David, but is also the very Son of God, has been made our King and our Lord—a fact to which the Old Testament prophets testified, and a fact that has been proven by His resurrection from the dead. Not only have I been given grace to obediently pursue my calling as an apostle, but you also have been called by Him, and He will empower you to pursue your calling just as He empowers me to pursue mine.

First of all, I want you to know that I am so grateful to God for your faith, which has been reported all over the world. With God as my witness I can tell you honestly that I never cease to bring you up to Him when I pray. And specifically I'm praying that He will make a way for me to come see you—please know that I have been planning this for a long time—because I really want to impart spiritual gifts to you, so that you may become established in Him. I can't wait to see the fruit you are going to produce. I've seen it in other churches already. I have a mission to preach the Gospel to every culture and ethnicity, so of course I can't wait to get to Rome to preach to you, too. It's going to be so encouraging for me and for you.

I'm not ashamed of the Gospel. It's the very power of God,

and it saves anyone who believes in God. First the Jewish people were given this insight, but now it's available to everyone. And for them, and now for you, from the beginning to the end, it is all received *by faith*. Habakkuk wrote of this very thing in the Old Testament: "It's by faith that one is made righteous." Now, I've already briefly described the Gospel, but what I want to do in this letter is give you the full picture of what this Gospel entails. And to understand this *Good News*, first you need to understand the bad news.

Because the fact is, mankind has had a problem ever since the Fall of Adam, and that problem is called *unrighteousness*, that is to say, *ungodliness*; and the wrath of God is eternally directed toward all unrighteousness. People who are unrighteous have no excuse for their unrighteousness, because everything that we could ever need in order to come to the knowledge of God has already been shown to us. From the green grass to the blue sky, everything that God made testifies to His existence, and therefore also testifies to His supreme power and authority. So, every unrighteous person down through the ages has somehow known that God was there behind the scenes. And yet they neither glorified Him nor showed Him gratitude. Their hearts and minds became vain and hollow; they allowed themselves to become spiritually stupid. They talked themselves into believing that they knew best, but they were complete buffoons. Instead of humbly seeking to find what God is like, they invented their own ideas, even going so far as to make images of various animals, and to worship them as if they were God! They went further than that. As they began to experience more and more repulsive cravings, they gave up on God's design for pure and holy sexuality. Women sexually engaged other women, and men sexually engaged other men. This is totally shameful behavior in God's eyes.

So unrighteousness abounded, in its many forms: all manner of sexual sin (that is, any sexual engagement outside the bonds of marriage—one man, one woman), sinister motives, greed, brazen rebellion, envy, murder, fighting, guile, mischievousness,

libel and slander, exceptionally anti-God attitudes, abuse, pride
and bragging, doing people wrong, disobedience to parents,
foolishness, breaking promises, heartlessness, cruelty,
ruthlessness. Now anybody who does these things deserves
death. But the unrighteous not only did these things, they
nodded in approval when others did them, too. And God
allowed these filthy choices, as well as their consequences. So, to
anyone who descends further and further into depravity, be
advised, He will let you have what you choose.

2 Now church, one of the reasons I felt the need to bring all
this up is that you need to get something straight: if all of these
people have become the objects of God's wrath, do you think it
will be any different for you if you do the same things? Not a
chance! If you sit in judgment of someone who is sinning, and
yet you're sinning just the same, you're going to be in for a rude
awakening, because you most certainly stand condemned. Just as
God was longsuffering with the unrighteous of previous
generations, He is longsuffering with you, too. But don't dare
take His kindness and mercy for granted. It's not there to take
advantage of, it's there to make you realize He's waiting for you
to get right with Him! If you don't repent of your hard heart,
there will be no solace for you on Judgment Day. If I can say it
the way David said it, "He will repay each and every person
according to what he has done." What will our rewards be?
Eternal life for the one who is continually faithful in doing good;
epic catastrophe for those who are only out for themselves and
never do turn from unrighteousness.

All of this is true regardless of whether you're a Jew or a
Gentile, because God ultimately makes no moral distinction
based on titles and customs. Try to understand how God looks
at Jews and Gentiles. The Jews have the Law of Moses, and they
are judged by it when they break it. But the Gentiles do not have
that Law, and yet they prove that they understand God's
unwritten law when they instinctively do right. Their law is one
that is written on their hearts. And when they sin, they break
that law, and their own conscience convicts them. So you see,

everyone is technically on an equal playing field before God, and whatever set of rules you are playing by, living a sin-free life is the object of the game. And mark my words, there is a day coming when God will judge every secret thought.

Now let me directly address the Jewish contingent of the church there in Rome for a moment. Some of you think that simply because you have Jewish blood and follow the Jewish customs—in particular, circumcision—that you are better than your Gentile brothers and sisters. And you don't mind telling everybody that you feel that way. Well, let me correct that. That kind of boasting is unjustified. You can't assume that you should be a teacher just because you have the Law of Moses. If you're teaching people not to commit adultery, but you yourself are committing adultery, you have no business trying to instruct anyone in the ways of the Lord. The same is true for any other kind of sin. Purify yourselves and keep the true law of God before you even think of "helping" those who don't know as much. Isaiah spoke of you when he said, "It's your fault that the Gentiles are blaspheming God."

I know that what I'm about to say is a totally radical thought for those of you who are Jewish—and don't forget, I'm Jewish, too—but we've got to shift the paradigm. We have always thought that what makes a Jew a Jew is Jewish ethnicity and Jewish custom. (In other words, I'm a Jew because I was born Jewish and because I keep the Law of Moses.) But God is revealing, through His Son, a new understanding of what it means to be Jewish. A true Jew is not one who has a particular type of DNA, nor is it one who gets himself circumcised. No, a true Jew is one who is a Jew inwardly, one who has a circumcised heart. And that doesn't happen merely by following the Law, but by yielding completely to the Spirit of God.

3 Now, you may be asking, "Was there even any point to this whole Judaism thing? Is there any benefit to being an ethnic Jew?" Well, yes, actually there is. See, it was to the Jewish people that the complete revelatory Word of God was delivered. They stewarded that revelation until such time as God saw fit to reveal this new layer: namely, Jesus. And even if some of the Israelites forsook the Law, does that make God any less faithful? Of course not. God's word would prove true even if everyone else were a liar. As it is written, "You'll be proven innocent because everything You say will be judged righteous."

Yet others might reason, "It seems like our sin leads God to do more good. So it's unfair to punish us for that sin. Let's sin more so God will get more glory." That's hogwash, and I won't even dignify such an evil line of thinking with a response. People who think that way will get what they deserve.

So, Jews are no better than Gentiles, and Gentiles are no better than Jews. The writers of the Old Testament have already said as much: "Nobody is righteous. Nobody! Nobody seeks God on his own. Nobody does good deeds of his own power and volition. Instead, their mouths utter filth and cursing, just like a snake produces venom. They have turned away from what's good and pursued what's evil. They are wretched and deceitful, they despise peace and value violence, and they clearly do not fear God." And the Law of Moses really doesn't change anything, because you can't be transformed from unrighteous to righteous just by following it. The Law is nothing more than a mirror, showing you how bad you are.

So that's the bad news: we've all sinned, we've all fallen short of the mark, we're all ineligible to experience God's glory, there's nothing we can do to fix ourselves, the Law of Moses can't even help us with this problem, and if we can't be changed, we're going to get scorched by the wrath of God. Bad news indeed! But that's why the Good News is good. So let me lay it out for you.

The Good News, the Gospel of Jesus Christ, is this: God has now made a way for us to be changed from unrighteous to righteous! How? As I said before, it's all *by faith*. That is, trusting in Jesus to cleanse you from sin and empower you to live a life that is pleasing to God. Now, how is this transformation accomplished on God's end?

Step 1: Propitiation. This means that the blood of Jesus

placated, or satisfied, God's wrath. After God had allowed centuries of sin to go unpunished, He sent Jesus to take our place and take our punishment. *Step 2: Redemption.* God bought us out of slavery to sin by paying a ransom; the price was the life of His Son. *Step 3: Justification.* Because Jesus took our guilt upon Himself, we are given a not-guilty verdict in the courtroom of eternity. *Step 4: Righteousness.* Our justification directly results in our right standing with God.

Because God does all the work in this process, there is absolutely no room for any of us to boast. He chose to demonstrate His righteousness and justice in this way. It's not because of something we did that we are made righteous. It's only by what He did. It's not by works of the Law. It can only be received by faith. God is God over the Jews and Gentiles, and both must come to Him by faith. Surely some will want to ask whether this invalidates the Law of Moses. Actually, no. On the contrary, it's only by faith that the Law can be fulfilled.

4 Let me digress for a minute, because I want to illustrate that point. Consider Abraham. Was he justified by works or by faith? Well the Bible says he "believed God, and because of that faith, God credited him with righteousness." That would be like God depositing money in his checking account. Abraham's faith gave him a credit. Now, could he have been credited, could he have been *given* this righteousness if he had worked for it? No. That contradicts the very definition of *working*. If you *work* for something, you *earn* a wage; you can only be *given* something if you did not *earn* it. Just like Abraham, when we believe in Jesus, we are justified, and our faith is credited to us as righteousness. It's given, not earned. David echoed the same thought when he said, "When God forgives people and no longer counts their sin against them, they're so happy."

So Abraham was justified by faith. When? After he was circumcised or before? Before! So this credit, this righteousness, this blessing is clearly not directly connected to the rite of circumcision. No, when Abraham got himself circumcised, that was simply a sign of what had already happened in his heart. But since he was also circumcised, he became the archetype of faith for *all* of us today, both for the uncircumcised and the circumcised. If you're uncircumcised, yet believe in Jesus, Abraham is your father. If you're circumcised, and you also believe in Jesus, Abraham is your father, too. Just as God told him, "I will make you the father of *many* nations." That means not only the nation that descended from his grandson, Israel (that is, Jacob), but also people of every ethnicity who put their trust in Jesus. (So, you see, it wasn't through the Law that Abraham and his children received the promised inheritance. It was by a faith that resulted in righteousness. If we could inherit that promise by following the Law, then there would be no point to faith and no value in the promise. Instead, the Law is merely a tool that points out our sin and convicts us of it.)

Look at the persistence of Abraham's faith, too. Remember how he was 100 years old, and his wife, Sarah, was way past the age of bearing children? Nevertheless Abraham was totally convinced that God would keep His promise that he would have many descendants. He never lost hope, although at times it looked hopeless. And he kept praising God for it. And God counted that faith as righteousness.

People of God, that wasn't just written down so the ancients could have an account, that story was written down as a testimony for us! So that we could understand that, for all times, God justifies the one who has faith. And that faith must be in His Son, Jesus, who died for our sins, and was resurrected to give us new life.

5 Okay, let me get back to my main point. I was talking about how God transforms us from unrighteous to righteous. And I had said that because Jesus served as propitiation, we also have redemption, justification, and righteousness. Well, guess what, even more blessings come after that! Let me explain.

Step 5: Peace. Because we are righteous, we have an unexplainable peace. We know that we no longer need to fear His wrath, and that brings a great comfort to our spirits. Jesus gives us access to God's grace, by faith, and through it we look forward to experiencing His glory.

Step 6: Reconciliation. Since we're at peace with God, there's now nothing stopping us from entering back into relationship with Him. Nothing stands between you and God! Hallelujah! You are reconciled to right relationship with God, the kind of fellowship that you were created for, the kind of fellowship that He had with Adam and Eve before the Fall.

And here's the really amazing part about reconciliation. God provided that reconciliation to us when we were at our worst. Dying for a *good* person is not unheard of, although even that level of selflessness is not common. But He died for *evil* people! The love He showed was not like the love of a parent or grandparent, feeling sorry for us because He had such a close connection to us. Totally to the contrary, at that point, He was not yet our Father! We were His enemies! We were just as putrid to Him as the Philistines or the Egyptians or the Sodomites were back in the day. And yet it was under these circumstances that Christ died for us. Amazing!

Step 7: Salvation. Understand this. Salvation is on the other side of the coin from reconciliation. Our reconciliation is accomplished through Jesus' death; our salvation is accomplished through Jesus' resurrection. Salvation from what? From His wrath, of course. But more than that, when I say *salvation* I really mean *wholeness.* We are restored to the fullness of life that Adam and Eve experienced in the garden. Jesus conquered sin, sickness, and death, and in Him we are made whole! I get so excited just thinking about the goodness of God!

Now, maintaining a confident expectation of a salvation like this doesn't just magically happen out of nowhere. That kind of hope is developed as we endure various trials and tribulations. When you encounter real tribulation, don't freak out and don't give up. Respond to it with joy. Because as you faithfully endure the difficult pressing of that hard place, you will find yourself becoming more and more steadfast. And at the end of the trial, you will be proven. That's a true confidence, because you know He's brought you through something. Those who find this kind of confidence have a real hope that cannot fail.

Step 8: No Condemnation. Condemnation is the opposite of justification—a guilty verdict is the opposite of a not-guilty verdict—so, of course, if we are justified, then we are, by definition, not condemned. Allowing this truth of "no condemnation" to settle in your spirit is important, and I want to elaborate on it a bit.

You have to understand the correlation between Adam and Jesus. Because Adam was disobedient and sinned, a judgment of death came upon mankind. That judgment of death was in effect from the time Adam sinned to the time God gave the Law to Moses. Everyone was affected by it. Even people who never broke a direct commandment of God were still sinning. They just didn't have the Law to tell them so. When the Law came, it brought condemnation, because now when people sinned, they knew exactly what they were doing wrong. As descendants of Adam, the sin gene has been passed down to us, too. It's part of our spiritual DNA from birth, and it results in condemnation and death. Jesus, on the other hand, did not inherit the sin gene, because His Father was God, not man. Furthermore, He was completely obedient, and did not ever sin. Thus, He was completely sinless when He went to the cross, which was the only way He could have been an acceptable substitutionary sacrifice for us. Through His death and subsequent resurrection, we have a new claim on life.

So Adam's disobedience made us sinners by nature, and his sin brought condemnation to us all; but Christ's obedience made us righteous, and His act of righteousness made justification and newness of life available to us all.

Now then, the Law of Moses was given in order to cause sin to increase, in the sense that people now had a measuring stick with which to demonstrate how sinful they were, and yet they still sinned. But now, anywhere sin exists, grace exists to a much greater degree. Whereas, prior to Jesus, *sin* held all of the power, and led to *death*; now *grace* holds all of the power, and it leads to *righteousness*, resulting in eternal life.

6 I know what some of you are thinking. You're thinking that if sin is always eclipsed by grace, maybe the thing we should do is just sin more, so we can maximize the grace we receive from God. No! No! No! Believe me it doesn't work that way! That line of so-called "logic" is as far from sound as it can be. You are vile if you adopt that kind of theology!

Please get this. Being baptized into Christ Jesus means being baptized into His death. And when you come out of the water, you are also raised to newness of life by the power of His resurrection! You can't have one without the other. Grace frees us from both the *guilt* of sin and the *power* of sin. You can't just accept your not-guilty verdict without also accepting the power that God gives you to walk sin-free! If we are dead to sin, how in the world could we possibly continue to live in it? You can't! Period!

Jesus only had to die once, and His resurrection proved His power over death. The sinful person you used to be was crucified with Christ. And in that, you were freed from your former slavemaster, sin. Sin no longer has power over you, you have power over it! Start acting like it! Don't give sin any wiggle room to gain a foothold in your life. If we died with Him, we should be living with Him, too. So stop presenting yourself to sin as if you're at its beck and call; it's not in charge anymore! Instead, start presenting yourself to God so that He can have His way with you. That's the way to righteousness.

Again church, don't adopt an attitude that is loose toward sin because you somehow think you can get away with it in the grace covenant. That's not the idea at all. You're just playing Russian Roulette with God's mercy; make no mistake, His wrath is in one of those chambers.

In the end, it's all about obedience. Whomever you obey, that's who your master is. If you obey sin, sin is your master and you are its slave; the end of that scenario is death. But if you obey God, God is your Master and you are His slave; the end of that scenario is righteousness and life. Obviously the second scenario is better, and thank God that's the one you've chosen.

You used to present your bodies as slaves to sin. Now you should be presenting them as slaves to righteousness, because that's what you are. You've been set free from sin. When you were slaves to sin, righteousness couldn't call the shots of your life, and you produced fruit that you were ashamed of. But if you've been set free from sin and have become a slave of God, you will begin to bear a new kind of fruit that is pleasing to Him. You've heard that fruit called by many names: love, joy, peace, patience, kindness, self-control, and on and on. Those are all facets of the same fruit. That fruit is called *holiness*. And in the end, if you follow through on bearing that fruit, eternal life will be yours.

I can't emphasize this enough: if sin is your boss, the wages you earn will be death; but if you truly receive God's free gift of grace offered through Jesus, then He will empower you to overcome sin and you will be rewarded with eternal life.

7 So, through Jesus we are freed from sin. But that's not all; we are also freed from the Law of Moses. In both cases, it's the death of our old self that makes this freedom possible, because if our old self still lives, both the Law and sin maintain control and authority.

Let me illustrate what happens to us when we are freed from the Law. Imagine that you and the Law are a married couple. You're the wife and the Law is the husband. Now your husband, the Law, really makes your life miserable. You just can't get any peace or happiness while you're living with him, because he simply expects more out of you than you can provide. That's when you notice Jesus. You just know that Jesus would be the perfect husband for you, and you begin to pine after Him. There's only one problem. You're married, and there's no way you can ditch the Law and get with Jesus. That would be adultery. What would be ideal is for your husband to die. Then you would be free to marry Jesus, and life would be a bed of roses.

But that's not what happens. God never does kill the Law. Instead, He pulls a total 180. The Law doesn't die, *you* die!

Because you're dead, you are freed from the covenant of marriage—just as free as if your husband, the Law, had been the one who died. Now you're free to marry Jesus (figuratively speaking). And what's the purpose of that marriage? To bear fruit to God. Nothing has changed since God first told Adam and Eve to be fruitful and multiply. Except now we're talking about spiritual offspring, not natural children. The Church, who is the Bride, is to become intimate with her Groom, Jesus, in order to produce spiritual offspring that may be presented back to God the Father. And that spiritual offspring, that fruit, as I've already said, is *holiness*. The purpose of your life is to have spiritual intimacy with Jesus so that you can bear the fruit of holiness to God!

What a transformation! What a rescue! When you were married to the Law, you were intimate with sin and the spiritual offspring you produced was death. Thank God He made a way for us to begin producing the right kind of fruit!

So, we're free from the Law. Does that mean the Law was bad? No. The Law is the standard of perfection. How could it be bad? It shows us what is right and wrong, and it convicts us when we don't measure up. How could I have known I was covetous, for example, if the Law had not said, "Thou shalt not covet"? So, though the Law is good, sin was able to use that good Law to its own evil ends, arousing in me desires contrary to the Law. Sin actually became empowered when I began to learn the Law. Instead of the Law leading me to life, sin grabbed hold of the reins and led me to death.

It's not the Law, which is good, that leads to death. It's the sin activated by the Law. See, we all come into this world with a sin factory inside us. That factory only knows how to produce sin. And that sin factory doesn't go away, even after we begin to believe in Jesus. We will always have the capacity to sin, right up until our dying day. Jesus' sacrifice does not eliminate our capacity to sin. Grace frees us from *the guilt of sin* and *the power of sin*, but not *the capacity to sin*. We are given a not-guilty verdict, and we are empowered to beat the sin factory, every time.

Unfortunately, most of us allow the sin factory to beat us from time to time—and I include myself in this. My sins are less egregious and fewer and further between than they used to be, but sometimes I still let the sin factory get the better of me. For example, maybe one day I notice some pride in my thinking, or maybe another day I show some impatience or frustration with a brother. I can't stand it when that happens! I don't want to be doing those things. When I sin like that, I know it's not the Spirit of God within me that's acting, but the sin factory. I'm allowing it to produce, even though I don't have to allow it, since I have the power through Jesus to beat it every time. Nevertheless, when I sin, in spite of my strong desire to please the Lord, I'm actually proving that the Law is good.

So there's a war going on inside me. The sin factory versus the Holy Spirit. I serve God by the power of the Holy Spirit. But occasionally I find myself serving sin by letting my carnal desires hold onto the power. This is such a troublesome burden! I want to be free 100% of the time! How can I get to that place?! I need help!

Lift up your eyes, saints! Here comes Jesus! When you find yourself in this position, just gaze up at Him and fall upon His mercy. Get on your face and cry out to Him to complete the work of making you more like Him, and then get up from that place and walk on, trusting that He will do it! The person who maintains this posture of repentance has no need to carry guilt and shame! **8** Because if you walk according to the Spirit, and not according to the flesh, you show yourself to be "in Christ Jesus." And in Him, there is no condemnation, ever!

Let me expand a bit on what I mean when I say "walk according to the flesh" and "walk according to the Spirit." I'm talking about a principle, or, if you like, an impulse. Actually, two competing principles or impulses. When we follow the principle or impulse of God (or, we might say, when we walk according to the law of the Spirit of Life, which is found in Christ Jesus), then the other principle, the other impulse—the law of sin and death—has no power over us. The Law of Moses couldn't save us from the law of sin and death. But Jesus can, and does! When God sent His Son to earth, and He became human, He was able to take sin to the cross and kill it. The principle and impulse of sin is dead, if you'll let it stay dead. And now Jesus fulfills, on our behalf, every single requirement of the Law of Moses, that is if we follow the principle or impulse of God, if we walk according to the Spirit.

Now how do we know if we're walking according to the flesh or walking according to the Spirit? Well, whoever walks according to the flesh sets his mind on the things of the flesh, and whoever walks according to the Spirit sets her mind on the things of the Spirit. If your thinking is consistently carnal, you're headed for death! But if you fix your mind on Him, He will wash your thoughts clean and put you on the path to life and peace.

Let me reiterate, to hold on to a carnal thought-life is to set yourself up in direct opposition to God. If you are thinking your own thoughts—the same kinds of thoughts worldly people think—you are not following the principle or impulse of God, and you cannot be pleasing to God! You are proving that you don't actually belong to Him because His Spirit is not in you. But if the Holy Spirit truly lives inside you, you will *not* continue on in the flesh. Now, I trust that you are His, and that as you read these words, any of you who are off track will allow Him to correct your course. If you're His, there is absolutely nothing forcing you to continue on in sin. So turn now!

Church, if I haven't made it plain enough already, let me make it painfully plain. I don't care if you *think* you're saved, I don't care if somebody told you you're saved, I don't care if you "made a decision" once upon a time to "accept Jesus." *If you continue to allow your carnal, worldly desires to control how you live life, you will die!* But, if, by the power of the Holy Spirit, you suffocate those desires and kill the actions they produce, you will live!

This is how we know we are the sons of God: by allowing His Spirit to lead us. The Holy Spirit confirms it to us. And if you have that assurance, then there is no reason to fear anything, nor to be re-enslaved. If you have been newly revealed as God's son, then you have every right to crawl up into God's lap and exclaim, "Daddy!"

Now, if we are His children, then we are His heirs, and we will receive an inheritance just as our big Brother, Christ, has. But if we're going to be glorified as He has been, then we should also expect to suffer as He did. Nobody enjoys suffering, but any persecution we suffer in this life pales in comparison to the glory we will experience in that Day. All of creation longs for that Day (not just us), because it will join us in enjoying the restoration of pure life and vibrancy—the effects of the Fall will be eliminated at that point. There's a groan within us, and within creation, that presses upon God to begin enacting His battle plan to defeat His enemies once and for all. When that happens, we will fully realize our destiny as sons, a destiny that has been guaranteed by the Spirit. This is the basis of hope. It wouldn't be hope if it were already here, now would it? No, but the Spirit within us assures us that it's all coming.

Not only does the Spirit guarantee our eternal destiny, He also helps us in the here and now. Even when we don't know what to pray, He prays for us and through us, sometimes even praying with more of a groan than a language. And we can be sure that what He prays for us is dead center of the will of God. After all, He is God! Not only that, Jesus is the embodiment of all God's authority, and He's petitioning the Father on our behalf, too! So, there's absolutely no doubt that God is for us! Which means that nobody can oppose us and win. If God was willing to give up His own Son for us, is there anything else He won't do to ensure that we make it?! No. He is behind the scenes at all times, pulling the strings to effect the most amount of good for those who are His (and those who He knows will eventually become His). He has laid out a destiny for everyone who loves Him. And that destiny is that we become like Him. He has called us, justified us, and glorified us.

So, once again, don't balk at persecution and tribulation. It cannot and will not separate you from the love of Christ. Even though right now we're like sheep heading to the slaughterhouse, the reality of the situation is, through Christ we're winning a decisive victory. There's nothing anyone can do to derail your destiny if you're a son of the living God—not people, not demons, nothing now and nothing later, nothing you will ever see in this life, not even a martyr's death. We are united to God in love forever because of Christ Jesus our Savior and King! Praise His Holy Name!

9 If you can "press pause" on this train of thought for a few minutes, I need to go on a tangent and explain more fully how the Gospel forces us to rethink what we mean when we say *Israel.* First of all, I have such a deep love and devotion to the Jewish people (after all, they are my kin) that I could almost volunteer to endure hellfire in order to save them. God has done so much for them—He called them His own, He showed them who He was, He made them promises and He has been faithful to fulfill every one, He gave them the Law, and He allowed them the privilege of ministering to Him; all of the fathers of the faith come from this heritage, as does Christ Himself, who is God in the flesh—it's so disappointing when I see some of them squander this manifold blessing.

See, any Israelite who does not receive Jesus forfeits all of God's promises to Israel. And conversely, any non-Israelite who receives Jesus taps into all of God's promises to Israel. Not everyone *called* Israel is actually Israel. Neither does every descendant of Abraham receive of God's promises. Let's remember what the Scriptures said about these things. First, God promised Abraham that he would father many nations, and that through his Seed (which we now know refers to Christ) the whole world would be blessed. Second, after the debacle with Hagar, God promised Abraham a son through Sarah. Third, God specified that the earlier promise of the Seed would come through Isaac. Fourth, God foreordained that Isaac's second-born son, Jacob (who was renamed Israel), would carry the Seed. This was God's sovereign choice and declaration to Isaac's wife, Rebecca, even though her firstborn son, Esau, had not yet done anything wrong. (This entire scenario just goes to show that

God is pulling all of the strings, calling and electing people not because of what they do, but because He knows best how to achieve His purposes.)

So, the children of the promise are not the natural descendants of Jacob, but rather the spiritual recipients of his Seed, Christ. It's not as though God is switching to "Plan B." Every promise made to Israel has been kept and is being fulfilled even today—through Jesus the Messiah.

Was God unfair to Esau? And is He now unfair to Israel? Is God unjust or unrighteous in how He conducts His business? No, that would be an impossibility. Remember, He said to Moses, "I will show mercy and compassion to whomever I choose." And Moses spoke the word of the Lord to Pharaoh, "I'm the One who put you in position just so I could demonstrate My power through you, so that My Name would be exalted in the earth." We can only conclude that God shows mercy to some and hardens the hearts of others. The mercy of God cannot be earned or chosen, it can only be received by faith.

Of course, the next question is, "Why does God find fault with those who oppose Him?" (It seems they're just doing what He is making them do.) But you really have no right to be asking such questions. The pot doesn't get to look up at the potter and ask, "Why did you make me this way?" The potter gets to decide which pots will be special and which will be common.

What if God just wanted to display His glory by patiently putting up with those who would eventually bear the brunt of His wrath, just so He could turn right around and pour His mercy into us, the pots He fashioned to hold His glory—those He called who are Jewish and those He called who are Gentiles? Didn't the Prophets foretell such a plan? God spoke through Hosea, "Those who are not my people, I will call *My People*. Those who are unloved, I will call *Beloved*. They will be the sons of God." And through Isaiah He said, "Israel numbers more than can be counted, but only a fraction will be saved. Without the Seed that God provided, they would be like Sodom and

Gomorrah. That's why He's going to be swift when He passes judgment on the others, who rejected the Seed."

Do you see it now? There are Gentiles who have stumbled onto righteousness, by faith, even though they weren't looking for it. And there are Jews who stumbled themselves right out of the promise, because they were trying to *earn* its fulfillment by what they did rather than receiving it from God as a gift, by faith. And Christ Himself is the Rock in their path that made them stumble. Isaiah wrote about that, too: "I'm going to place a Rock in Zion. Whoever believes in Him will not be ashamed."

10 Church, I want all of the Jewish people to be saved, about as much as I want anything. They are enthusiastic about God and His ways, but they do not understand how to please Him. They're trying to make themselves righteous by following the Law, but they're not actually submitted to God's true path to righteousness. It's their Messiah who actually fulfills the Law on our behalf when we trust fully in Him to do it.

Moses said that anyone who obeys the Law will live. But he also said that the commandment of God was not so high we couldn't reach it, and it's not buried so deep we can't uncover it. He said, "It's very near! Even in your heart and in your mouth!" In other words, the Messiah is not merely up in heaven, aloof and inaccessible to us. And He sure ain't still dead in the ground! He lives in your heart, and from there He wells up into the things you say.

This is the message of faith that I am preaching to you! If you believe in your heart that God raised Him from the dead, and your genuine confession is that Jesus is the Lord of your life, He will empower you to live a life that is pleasing to Him; you will be made righteous and you will be made whole. God's work of making us righteous is performed in our hearts, and His work of bringing us to the fullness of power and authority is brought about when we continually declare what aligns with His Word and His Will. This is true whether one is Jew or Gentile: "Whoever believes in Him has no reason to fear shame. Whoever calls on His name, leaning completely on His mercy, will be saved." (So said the Prophets.)

Now, the Jewish people are not going to be able to call on Jesus if they don't believe in Him, and they're not going to be able to believe in Him if they don't hear about Him, and they're not going to hear about Him if nobody tells them about Him. So, right now, I'm calling on all of you to begin to preach the good news of Jesus Christ. Then you will be the ones the Prophets referenced when they said, "Even though those who travel far and wide to preach the Gospel end up with dirty feet, those feet are actually beautiful in God's sight because of the purpose they have served."

In order for people to believe, they have to hear the faith-producing message, and that message is the Good News of Jesus Christ. Of course, not everyone you preach to will believe. Isaiah foreshadowed that fact, saying, "They're not all believing our report, Lord!" And remember, there's no excuse for not believing. The Israelites have actually heard this message already. David declared that even the heavens have "proclaimed a message that has gone out to the ends of the earth." The Lord spoke through Moses, saying, "I'm going to arouse jealousy and anger in you by doing something through a bunch of other people." Isaiah confirmed this word when he spoke of Gentile believers: "People found Me that weren't even looking for Me." Meanwhile, the Israelites continued to be obstinate and disobedient despite God's mercy.

11 Then did God turn His back on His people? No! I'm a perfect example. I'm a direct descendant of Israel, through his son, Benjamin. But I'm also a child of the promise through Abraham's Seed, the Christ. You can be both; I'm living proof. Do you remember when Elijah expressed his concern about Israel's destiny? He said, "God, they have destroyed all of Your sacred people and demolished all of Your sacred places. I'm the only one left who honors You, and they're coming for me, too!" But God knew the end, and assured him, saying, "Don't worry. I have reserved for Myself a fraction of the people, who have not descended into idol worship." We are seeing the fulfillment of that word now. The remnant of Israel—saved by grace, not by works—is gaining access to the promise, according to the election of God.

So, the Jewish people as a whole were not able to grasp what they were going after. But the elected fraction seized it, while everyone else remained blind to it. The Scripture says, "Since their blessings have caused them to become complacent, self-sufficient, and rebellious, God has closed their eyes and ears, bent their backs over, and removed from them all access to His new workings."

Have the Israelites gone so far that they're beyond all hope? Not at all. God has used the fact that they stumbled to bring the offering of salvation to everyone else. This will make the Israelites jealous, and eventually we will see many of them turn back to God. If the Gentiles are happy about the benefits they've received because of Israel's rejection of the Messiah, imagine how exciting it will be for them when they see the remnant begin to accept Him. (My apostolic mission is primarily to the Gentiles, and this dynamic I've been describing is something I'm supposed to be emphasizing.)

Let me try to illustrate everything I've been saying here. Imagine two olive trees, one cultivated and one wild. The cultivated tree is named *Israel*, and the wild tree is named *Not-Israel*. What has happened is that certain segments of the tree called *Israel* did not continue in the faith by believing in Jesus as their true fulfillment of the Mosaic Law. Because of this unbelief, these branches have been cut off from the *Israel* tree. But then several branches from the tree called *Not-Israel* heard the message about Jesus and believed. These have been removed from *Not-Israel* and grafted into *Israel*. Thus, Israel is Israel. The tree is the tree. It's not a new tree, it's not a different tree, it's not a replacement tree, but it is a tree that has been reshaped to include branches that weren't there before, and to exclude branches that were there before.

Once again, there's no justification for bragging about being part of this tree. Nobody earns a place in it. Faith by grace grafts you in, and unbelief outside God's grace cuts you off. And it's not like you're one of the roots, anyway. You're just a branch. The roots—that is, the patriarchs—were holy. Because the roots were holy, the branches are holy. If some of the natural branches have been cut off, you can be, too! (God is just as severe as He is kind.) Not only that, if those who have been cut off come to receive Christ by faith, they will be re-grafted in. Indeed, it will be much easier for them because they were already a part of the tree to begin with.

So, parts of Israel experienced a blinding in order to make room for all the Gentiles who would believe. When God is finished grafting in the Gentiles, we can expect more Jews to be re-grafted in. This is the way that all Israel is saved—the whole tree. This should humble you, not make you conceited. God has a marvelous plan for all of His people, not just you. You used to be disobedient, and God showed you mercy. Now they're being disobedient, but God's going to show them mercy, too. As it is written, "The Deliverer will come out of Zion, and He will remove all ungodliness from Jacob. My covenant is the removal of sins." God will not dishonor the holy patriarchs by chopping down the whole tree. He's not in the business of rescinding His gifts and callings. Instead, He's allowed us all to descend into disobedience so He could turn right around and show mercy to us all.

Do you see yet how unfathomable God's mercy is?! His wisdom and knowledge are such a mystery, there's no way we could ever expect to fully comprehend what He's up to. Nobody knows exactly what He's thinking. Nobody can give Him input. You haven't contributed anything to Him, and He doesn't owe you anything. Everything originated from Him, everything is made and sustained through Him, and everything will be subjected to Him. It is all for His glory alone! Amen! (Tangent over.)

12 What's the logical conclusion of everything I've said so far in this letter? If the tree is holy, you've got to be holy in order to be part of it. Start presenting yourself to God so that He can have His way with you. Stop walking according to the flesh, and start walking according to the Spirit, so that the promise of no condemnation will be fulfilled in you. Be holy! I'm begging you! This is what it means to worship God acceptably! Walking in purity is not optional. Only those who allow God to do the work of making them holy will prove to be heirs of the promise. You can't go on thinking and acting the way the world does. You must allow Him to transform you. In other words, God's solution to the problem of unrighteousness—propitiation, redemption, justification, righteousness, peace, reconciliation, salvation, no-condemnation—is all contingent on taking the last step…

Step 9: Sanctification. Sanctification is the process of becoming holy. Now, I've been talking about "steps" in a "process," but actually, Steps 1-8 all happen simultaneously. Only this ninth step is a true process, developing progressively over a lifetime. When you are born again, you become a child of God. Propitiation, redemption, justification, righteousness, peace, reconciliation, salvation, and no-condemnation are automatically yours. Nevertheless, you are merely a spiritual newborn, which means you still have to grow up. You have to come to the place where you are spiritually mature enough to bear the fruit of holiness to God.

Okay, I think I've made it clear that we need to be holy in order to please God and become heirs of the promise. So let me take some time now to give you some specifics on what a life of holiness should look like. First of all, we need to make sure that we are using the gifts that God has given us in a way that actually achieves His purposes. Since we, all together, make up one body, it follows that our various members will have different functions, so that we can all work together according to God's master plan. Those who have gifts that people perceive as more impressive can't think too highly of themselves. That gift was given. You had nothing to do with it. It's just one of many gifts that we all need in order for our church body to function efficiently. So if you've been given the gift of prophecy, just prophesy and get out of the way without drawing attention to yourself. If you have a special gift of serving, serve well. If you've been given the gift of teaching, teach. If you're especially gifted with encouragement, encourage; giving, give; leadership, lead; mercy, be merciful.

In addition, we've got to love people. I mean really love people, not just say that we do. Loving people means showing them preferential treatment. You have to temper your own desires and preferences and give consideration to the desires and preferences of others. Heap honor on your brothers and sisters in Christ.

Anything that displeases God should disgust us, and anything that pleases God should resonate strongly in our spirits. Be diligent regarding the things of the Lord. Burn white hot on the inside. Submit yourself fully to Him. Let the hope of your salvation bring you joy. Let the trials of life do their work of building up your perseverance. Remain committed to prayer. Give generously to holy brothers and sisters who have needs. Open the doors of your home for fellowship. Ask God to bless anyone who does you wrong. Cry with each other, and laugh with each other. Be unified. Be humble, not proud. Go after God's wisdom, not your own. Don't operate on the principle of revenge. Wait and see what God will do. He's already said He would take care of it. Instead, be so upstanding that everyone takes note. Don't be the one to break the peace. "Feed your enemy when he's hungry, and give him a drink when he's thirsty. That'll teach him a lesson." Then sit back and watch good crush evil right in front of your eyes.

13 You must submit to every authority that is over you. That includes the government, the workplace, the church, and so on. (Yes, that even includes paying your taxes.) All authority comes from God, and He has delegated that authority all around the world. Not every authority figure is godly, but they are all "from God." What they do with their authority is between them and God. You just make sure you're submitted, otherwise you're actually rebelling against God. As a general principle, if you do right, you won't have to fear your authority figures anyway. If you do wrong, you *should* fear them, because they are there to straighten you out. So do right to avoid punishment, but also just do right because it's right.

Don't get yourself in debt. The only thing you should owe anybody is love. All of the commandments that deal with how people should relate to each other—commandments against murder, adultery, theft, covetousness, and so on—are totally encapsulated in this one principle: love your neighbor as yourself. Love can't hurt anybody. Therefore, it perfectly fulfills the Law.

And another thing. We've got to wake up and smell the coffee. We are progressing toward the end of time. Things are not going to just continue on as they are doing now. Judgment Day is closer today than it ever has been. Now, we are children of the light, not children of the darkness. You have to start acting like "day" people, and stop participating in the stuff "night" people do: drunkenness and the out-of-control behavior it leads to, any kind of sexual sin that trespasses God's set boundary (that boundary is a marriage between one man and one woman), even jealousy and selfish discord. Church, cover yourself with the Lord Jesus as if He's a garment. Do not fulfill the lusts of the flesh. In fact, take every precaution to keep temptation at arm's length.

14 We, as the Church, need to do everything we can to remain unified. We do not accept behavior that has been clearly forbidden by God, but when it comes to those things that God has not expressly weighed in on, we should be sensitive, and even deferential to brothers and sisters who hold different convictions. For example, some may be convicted in their spirits that Christians shouldn't be eating certain foods, while others may not hold the same conviction. Some may be convicted that certain days are holier than others, warranting special activities, while others may not hold the same conviction. The Holy Spirit operates differently in different people. What may work for one may not work for another. You've got to be obedient to the prompting of the Lord and not follow somebody else's rules.

Everything we do is done unto God, so make sure you're doing what you sense in your heart He is asking you to do. If we eat, we eat unto the Lord, and if we observe a day as being holy, we do that unto the Lord, too. If we refrain from those activities, we have the Lord in mind as well. Whether we live or die, we belong to the Lord, and He died and rose again to become the Master of everything, dead and alive. Each of us will give an account. A day is coming when we will all stand before the Judgment Seat of Christ. As it is written, "Every knee will bow to Me, and every tongue will confess that I am God." So don't judge each other, but don't cause each other to stumble either.

I'm convinced that when it comes to food, nothing is off limits. I believe Jesus Himself has put my mind at ease about this. But if you think otherwise, yet you go ahead and eat what you believe you shouldn't eat, then you're not eating in faith, and that's going to be sin in your case. And if you're around someone who is convicted about certain foods, don't eat those foods around them. That's simply deferring to other folks' convictions for the sake of withholding offenses. It's a gesture of love to restrain yourself for the benefit of others. If you can't say "no" to something for someone else's sake, you're allowing a perceived freedom to become an actual stronghold. Don't let something that's good for you become bad for them. Don't tear down the work God is doing in someone else's life just because you want to eat or drink something in particular. God's kingdom isn't about what we eat. It's about righteousness, peace, and joy in the Holy Spirit. So don't eat meat or drink wine or do anything else if it's going to offend or weaken one of your brothers. Operate on the principle of faith, which is birthed out of the relationship between you and God. And don't find yourself entering into condemnation because you approved of something you shouldn't have. You'll be happier that way.

15 Even Jesus didn't get His own way. He had to endure all of the unwarranted attacks that people launched against God.

And that serves as a lesson for us now. So it's the least we can do to take each other by the hand, to consider others more highly than we consider ourselves, to encourage them in the Lord, to do everything we can to ensure their success. If we can be unified like that, God will receive glory.

I'm talking to the Jews, and I'm talking to the Gentiles. Stay together! Jesus came to the Jews first, and now He has come to the Gentiles, so that they, too, can praise Him for His mercy. God's master plan is available to anyone who believes! As it is written, "The Jews will praise the Lord among the Gentiles, and the Gentiles will rejoice and praise the Lord in return. Their hope is in Him, too." I'm praying and believing that God will give you all the peace, hope, and joy you can stand as you walk together! *Lord, You are so patient and kind. Grant that they may pursue You with one mind.*

Church, I am confident that you are doing well, and will continue to move forward in the things of God. You understand the core of what I've been communicating already, and you even have boots on the ground that are able to teach. I'm simply writing these things as a reminder. We all need to be reminded of the truth from time to time so that we don't lose sight of it. I'm trusting that this message will ignite a resurgence in your sanctification process. As an apostle to the Gentiles, it's my duty to encourage you this way. I've been preaching to people who have never heard the Gospel, all up and down the entire northeast quarter of the Mediterranean seaboard—from Jerusalem to Croatia—while the Lord confirms my ministry with signs and wonders. As it is written, "People who neither saw nor heard are starting to understand anyway." I'm excited about everything the Lord is doing through me, but I don't dare hold onto any of the credit. He's doing it all!

Unfortunately, all this work has prevented me from coming to you so far. But I'm finished ministering in that region now, so I don't think it will be long before I get to Rome. I do have to go to Jerusalem first. Some of the other churches took up a collection for the saints in Jerusalem, and I will be delivering it to them. The Gentiles are so grateful that the message about Jesus was sent to them from Jerusalem, they are more than happy to bless the church there financially. Anyway, once I finish that trip, my plan is to head to Spain, and I'm hoping to drop by Rome on my way. I'll need help for the journey, which I'm sure you'll provide, and I certainly want to be able to minister to you, and share the good news of Jesus Christ in person!

So, please pray fervently for me. Pray that the Lord protects me from the unbelievers in Jerusalem, that we may make an impact with our gifts and ministries there, that I will be able to come to Rome, and that we will enjoy each other when I get there. May the God of peace be with you all. Amen.

16 I'm trusting you to take care of Phoebe *[the lady delivering the letter]* while she's there, and to assist her with anything she feels led to do. She is a deaconess in the church in Cenchrea in southern Greece, and she has been faithful to me, and to many others.

I know several people living there in Rome. Please be sure to relay my greetings to all of them:

- Priscilla and Aquila, my partners in the work of God. They have actually risked their lives for me. I'm so grateful to them, as are all of the Gentile churches. Greetings also to all of those who meet in their house church.

- Epenetus, who was the first person in southern Greece to become a believer. Also, Mary, who worked tirelessly on our behalf. The same goes for Persis. Tryphena and Tryphosa, too.

- Andronicus and Junia, who, in my book, rank right at the top of the list of apostles. Indeed, they came to Christ before I did.

- Amplias and Stachys. I love them. Urbanus, another fellow worker in Christ. Apelles, who has been approved by Christ. Aristobulus and his whole household. Also Narcissus and his house. Herodion; he's kin to me. Rufus, who is marked by God, and his mother, who is like a mother to me.

- Asyncritus, Phlegon, Hermes, Patrobas, Hermas, and their congregation. Also Philologus and Julia, Nereus and his sister, Olympas, and all of their congregation.

Greet each other in love and holiness. All of the churches everywhere send their greetings as well.

Oh. I feel led to send one more warning. Take note of anyone that tries to stir up trouble by teaching something contrary to what you know to be right, and avoid those people. They're not actually serving the Lord. They're only out for themselves. Charm and flattery are the tools of their trades: deception and spiritual pickpocketing. You are an obedient people, and everybody knows it. Let's make sure we stay that way. It won't be long before Satan is crushed by the weight of the Almighty God. And you get to take part in stamping him out. May the grace of our Lord Jesus Christ be with you all. Amen.

My partner in ministry, Timothy, as well as my relatives, Lucius, Jason, and Sosipater all greet you. Gaius, my host (indeed, the whole church's host), says hello, too. As does Erastus, the city treasurer, and our brother, Quartus.

Hi, everybody, this is Tertius. I'm the one taking dictation for Paul. Blessings!

Now, to God, who alone is wise, who enables you to be obedient, thus establishing you in the faith—faith in Jesus Christ, originally a mystery, subsequently a prophecy, and now a reality—to Him be all glory through Jesus Christ. Forever. Amen.

Discussion Questions

WEEK 5: Romans 1-5

- What is humanity's problem? And what are the first eight parts of God's solution to this problem? Elaborate on each part.
- What does it mean to receive God's solution "by faith?"
- James told us we are justified by works (Jms 2:24), but Paul says we are justified by faith and not by works (Rom 3:28). Are these contradictory statements (as they seem to be on the surface)? Explain.
- Why did Paul include the "aside" of Romans 4?

WEEK 6: Romans 6-8

- The promise of "no condemnation" (Rom. 5:18, 8:1) is conditional. Romans 6 defines that condition. Explain.
- Define *grace*.
- The way we know if we're walking according to the flesh is if our minds are set on the things of the flesh. What sorts of things constitute "things of the flesh?" What is *your* mind set on?
- If your mind is set on the things of the Spirit, then you have no condemnation, and the Spirit bears witness from within you that God is your Daddy. Do you have that witness? Describe the joy of your relationship with Abba Father.

WEEK 7: Romans 9-11

- What does Paul mean when he says, "Not all Israel is Israel"?
- After coming to understand the context of Romans 9-11, do you think that Romans 10:9 is an ideal "formula" for salvation (as many make it out to be)? Is there a verse in Romans that might be more ideal?

- Explain the "two trees" analogy in your own words (Chapter 11).
- Given the message of this section, is there any room for Anti-Semitism in the Christian faith? *(Hint: the answer is "no.")* Explain.

WEEK 8: Romans 12-16

- Explain how the command to be holy in Rom 12:1 flows out of Romans 11 *and* Romans 8 *and* Romans 6.
- What commands from the "to-do lists" and "to-don't lists" in this section jumped out at you? What adjustments to your lifestyle is the Lord dealing with you to make right now?
- The context of Paul's message in Chapter 13 regarding submission to authority is the reign of the Roman Emperor, Nero, one of the most horrific periods of Christian persecution—public torture and execution—in history. How does this context inform your personal opinions about the necessity of submission to authority in your life (i.e., your home, your church, your workplace, your government authorities)?
- What is the overarching message of Romans? And how should that message impact your everyday life?

PAUL'S LETTER TO THE
GALATIANS

1 To the churches of Galatia,

From Paul (an apostle appointed by God and not by man) and all of the saints who are with me.

May the grace and peace of God be heaped onto you. He is the Father of our Lord Jesus Christ, the One who sacrificed Himself to wipe away our sins and enable us to overcome the world's temptations. It's God's will that we do just that. And He is the One to whom we give all the glory in all things. Amen.

Let me get right down to business. I am shocked that you are turning away so quickly from the pure Gospel to a different gospel. Of course, there is no other gospel, but many have come along who want to put their own spin on the truth and pervert the message. God called you into the grace of Christ. Don't allow anyone to call you out of it. As I've said before, if anyone preaches a gospel different from the one you received at the beginning, let him be cursed. That goes for anyone, even an angel from heaven—or even me! Anyone who distorts the Gospel message is only out to garner favor with people. Do I look like I care about pleasing people to you? Fat chance! I seek to please God in all I do, and I pay the price for it. But that's what the life of a slave of Christ looks like, and I'm okay with that.

The Gospel I delivered to you was not an invention of man. I didn't receive it from a mere mortal; I received it by direct revelation from Jesus Himself. You already know my story. I was a terrible person. I spent years climbing the ladder in the Jewish religious community, rising with the tide of Christian blood. I was more zealous than my contemporaries, and I had made it my mission to persecute and annihilate the Church. Then God arrested me! This God who had called me and separated me while I was still in my mother's womb, waited until the perfect time to reveal His Son to me and in me. I did a total 180, and began to pursue Him and His call for my life. That call was to preach the Gospel to the Gentiles. I didn't go ask anybody if that was what I was supposed to do. I knew it without a doubt, and I went out and started doing it.

Three years later I went to Jerusalem to meet Peter. I stayed with him 15 days. I also met James, the Lord's brother, there. They affirmed me and confirmed my message and mission, but even they did not articulate some gospel that differed from what I was already preaching. For the Gospel I preach and the Gospel they preach are one and the same. And they were the only two apostles I met at that time. (With God as my witness, this is the way it all went down.)

After that I went to Syria and the southern coast of Turkey. The believers in Judea, hundreds of miles away, still would not have recognized me at this point. They just kept hearing that this guy who used to hunt them down is now preaching the very Gospel he once tried to eradicate. Of course, they praised God for that. But my point is, I still wasn't getting my message from the top brass; they didn't even know me.

2 It wasn't until 14 years later that I returned to Jerusalem, this time with Barnabus and Titus. I went simply because the Lord told me to. I recounted to the trustworthy brothers there the message I had been preaching. I wanted to make sure everything I was saying was in alignment with what they were saying. After all, I definitely didn't want to be devoting my life to this cause in vain. Well, we *were* in agreement. In fact, we were even in agreement on the question of *circumcision*. Titus, who was an uncircumcised Gentile, felt no conviction to get himself circumcised, and all the leaders agreed that it was unnecessary for him to do so!

Now, the question of circumcision, which, I don't have to tell you, is one of the main issues within the Gentile-believer community right now, came about because a group of imposters weaseled their way into the fellowship and started propagating the idea that some of the Jewish rites should be added to *the Faith*. This false message preached by these fake Christians is nothing more than a tactic of the enemy to re-enslave those who have become free in Christ. But we didn't buy into their nonsense for one minute. We wanted to make sure that we preserved the pure Gospel for you.

Long story short, none of the leaders in Jerusalem who were held in high regard by the Church ever had anything to add to what I had been preaching. (Of course, the fact that they were regarded highly makes no difference to me. God doesn't have favorites.) In fact, they all recognized that I had been called as apostle to the Gentiles, just as Peter had been called as apostle to the Jews; this is simply the way God ordained our missions. And when James and Peter and John perceived the grace on my life, they agreed that Barnabus and I should go to the Gentiles while they concentrated on the Jews. The only thing they advised was that we remember the poor, and we wouldn't dare recoil from that mandate.

Then came my run-in with Peter. He had come to Antioch, and while he was there he mingled quite a bit with the Gentiles. But as soon as an envoy from James arrived, he withdrew from the Gentiles and only associated with the Jews. Falling prey to a classic "fear of man" scenario, he was worried about what the Jews would think of him. And Barnabus and some others joined him in this hypocrisy.

So, when I saw that they were not presenting the Gospel purely, I challenged them to their faces. This episode had brought condemnation on them, and I told them so. In front of everyone, I said to Peter:

You are a Jew who gave up the Jewish traditions in order to live like a Gentile. Why would you try to talk the Gentiles into adopting those same traditions in order to live like the Jews? We are Jews by birth, made privy to the path of righteousness in a way that Gentiles were not. Yet even we have come to believe in Christ Jesus, because He has revealed to us that nobody is justified simply by adhering to the Mosaic Law. Rather, one can only be made righteous by believing in Jesus to forgive and enable. Now, if the pure-hearted pursuit of Jesus causes us to be numbered among the sinners, that would mean that Jesus actually promotes sin. That's an impossibility! Just the other way around, it's the one who rebuilds the prison of legalism Jesus destroyed, who is in violation.

The Law never saved me; it condemned me, because I tried to keep it and yet still failed to attain righteousness. I had to reckon myself dead with respect to the Law in order to be counted righteous in God's eyes through Jesus. My faith in Jesus puts me in the position of being *in Him* and *with Him* in all things. That means when He was crucified, I was crucified right along with Him. It's not the old, natural, carnal me that calls the shots of my life. Nor is it the former, Law-keeping me. It's the Lord. My entire life—the totality of my thoughts, attitudes, and actions—is lived by faith in the Son of God, who loved me and gave Himself for me. To live my life according to the Law would be to render the grace of God ineffectual and meaningless. I'm not going to do that. If I could have attained righteousness, apart from the grace-through-faith principle, simply by keeping the commandments of the Mosaic Law, then Christ's death would have been pointless, wouldn't it?

3 Now I'm saying the same thing to you, Galatians! You fools! What kind of hocus pocus lured you away from the truth?

Shouldn't the picture we painted for you of the crucified and resurrected Jesus be enough to keep your faith on track? Answer me this: How was it that you received God's Holy Spirit, by the Law or by faith? By faith! Now having been saved by faith, do you really think you're going to move forward in the sanctification process by reverting back to the Law? Not hardly! All of the things of the Spirit are accessed through faith; none are accessed through the Law. Have the things you have suffered all been for nothing? Did God give His Spirit to you and work miracles in your midst because you followed the Law? No, it was because of your faith in Jesus.

The way you've attained righteousness is the same way Abraham did—through faith in what you heard. God spoke a Promise to him, and the Scripture says, "Abraham believed God, and his faith was credited to his spiritual account in the currency of righteousness." Now, Abraham is our model in this. Only those who have faith are heirs of Abraham. This includes you Gentiles. In fact, God spoke to Abraham about the inclusion of the Gentiles in the Promise when He said, "All the nations of the world will be blessed through you." Don't you see? Those who have *faith* are the ones who will receive Abraham's blessing.

Everyone who tries to live according to the Mosaic Law is under a curse. The Bible says it this way, "Failure to meet every requirement of the Law will result in a curse." Now, if it were possible to keep the Law perfectly, that would be one thing. But only Jesus could do that. It's impossible for the rest of us. Attaining righteousness by meeting all of the Law's requirements apart from faith? That's only an abstract, hypothetical pathway, not a real-life alternative. No, the only viable path to righteousness was prescribed by Habakkuk: "Those who live *by faith* are the ones deemed righteous." No one is justified by the Law!

The good news, *the Gospel*, is that Christ has purchased our freedom and effectively removed this curse-of-the-Law from us. He did this by taking the curse upon Himself in our stead. (Remember, the Scripture says, "Everyone who hangs on a tree is cursed.") Now, since the Law of Moses has been outflanked, we find ourselves backtracking to the original promise given to Abraham. In other words, Gentiles, too, may receive the blessing promised to Abraham, through Christ Jesus, since there is no Law-requirement (which was reserved for the Hebrews) standing in their way. *Anyone* who believes may receive the blessing of the Holy Spirit!

Just think in terms of normal everyday business practices. If you're in a contract with somebody, you can't just break it willy nilly. You would either have to show good cause in order to get out of it, or else pay some sort of penalty. Well, in this case, we're not talking about a contract that is merely difficult to break; we're talking about a covenant that is totally irrevocable. God's promise to Abraham is eternal and unchangeable. And that promise was made to Abraham "and to his Seed." Notice it doesn't say, "and to his seeds," as if it were referring to all of his physical descendants. No, it says it is "to his Seed," meaning "to Christ." So, anyone who is in Christ receives this inheritance. Now, the Mosaic Law, which, don't forget, was given 430 years later, can't undo the Promise and renegotiate the Covenant. Do you think God is going to suddenly write an addendum in fine print after the guy He's in covenant with is already in the grave? There's no way. So, if keeping the Law could make us heirs of the blessing, then we would not be inheriting it through faith in the Promise. But God's mode of delivering the blessing to Abraham was through his faith in the Promise.

Okay, well then what in the world was the purpose of the Law? God added the Law to the Promise simply as a way of giving the people documented proof that they were indeed sinful. But now that the Seed has come, and the Promise has been fulfilled, there is no need to look back at the Law, because it no longer convicts us. (Also, the Law was given to the middleman, Moses, because when you're dealing with a big group of people, a middleman is necessary. But God's Promise to Abraham was between one God and one man, and it needed no middleman. That's just one more distinction between the

Law and the Promise.)

So, God's Law and God's Promise are not in conflict with one another. God's Promise gives eternal life. God's Law, on the other hand, showed us that we didn't measure up, leading us to receive the mercy and grace of God by faith in the Promise. And that Promise has now been fulfilled in us who believe in Jesus Christ. The Law was our prison guard. It held us captive, while also protecting us until the time of our release. But the Law was also our schoolmaster, teaching us the standard of holiness, showing us that we couldn't attain it, and training us to look forward to the Christ. Once we graduated and God handed us our diploma of faith in Christ, we no longer needed the schoolmaster.

Now we are neither prisoners of the Law nor students of the Law. We are sons of God. *[That includes females, too, because "sons" is simply a way of saying that we are the ones who receive the inheritance.]* If we are baptized into Christ Jesus, then we are "in Him" just as if He were the clothes we wear. Being male or female has no bearing on whether one may be in Christ. Neither does it matter if you're a slave or a free man. It doesn't even matter if you're a Jew or Gentile, because the Law (that is, what defines Jewishness) has been rendered moot as we now trace the Promise from Jesus (backward right past the entire history of Israel) directly to Abraham. You who have faith in Christ are the direct spiritual descendants of Abraham, and the true heirs of God. Period.

4 Now, just because somebody's an heir doesn't mean he automatically has full access to the inheritance. A child who has not reached full maturity, for example, may be the rightful heir of the entire estate, and yet he technically has no more rights to it than a slave does. He has to subject himself to his guardians and the trustees of the estate until such time as he grows up and gains access to everything. That's how it was with us. We were minors, and, for all intents and purposes, slaves to the spiritual system of the world brought about by the Fall in the Garden. But at the appointed time, God sent His Son, born a human being, subject to the Law, in order to buy back out of slavery everyone under the Law, thereby securing our full legal status as sons of God. And the moment you became His sons, He sent the Spirit of *the* Son into your hearts, enabling you to address the Father tenderly and informally as "Daddy God!" Yes, Church, we are no longer slaves, but sons, heirs of God through Christ.

In the past, when you didn't know God, you were enslaved to the ways of the world. Now after having come to know God (or, at least, having been known by Him), are you seriously going to turn around and subject yourself again to the world's doomed system? Do you really think that observing certain days or months or seasons or years in a ritualistic fashion is going to bring you closer to God? I'm beginning to get the feeling that everything I've done for you has been a big waste of time and energy. I'm really pretty concerned for your eternal future.

Folks, you need to do what I did when it comes to these Jewish customs: scrap them all. I became just like you when I did that, disencumbered of religious rituals. Unfortunately, since you have added to your own faith the very burdens I laid down, you're where I was before I became like you. Now you need to become like me in the way that I became like you back then.

I remember so fondly the times we had when I first preached the Gospel to you. You were so eager to hear and receive, and even though my physical condition was a nuisance to me and a distraction to you, you nevertheless honored me and treated me as if you were receiving my message from an angel, or even from the Lord Himself. I have no doubt you would have taken your eyeballs out of your head and given them to me, if you had thought it would help. I wish you still felt that way about me. It seems like you've almost totally written me off, simply because I speak the truth!

These false teachers are zealous about winning you over to their false teaching. They've positioned themselves between you and me so that the truth may be blocked and you will fall for their lies—hook, line, and sinker. But zeal is only a good thing when it's zeal for the truth. My little children, I am going through labor pains for you now a second time, this time to see Christ fully formed within you. Then I can really be at peace about the situation. I was excited that you had been birthed at the start, but with what I'm hearing now, I just don't have a full assurance that you're His. How I wish I could be there so I could talk to you face to face, and maybe stop the bleeding!

You think you want to keep the Law? You wouldn't if you understood the position it puts you in. Let me explain.

Abraham had two sons, one by a maidservant who had little in terms of rights or freedom, and another by a woman with a full range of rights and freedom. The son he had by the maidservant was birthed out of Abraham's striving, in the natural, to produce a solution to his problem. But the son he had by the free woman was a miracle baby, a supernatural fulfillment of God's Promise.

Well, these two births, these two women and their sons, symbolically represent the two covenants. On the one hand, we have the covenant of the Law given at Mount Sinai. That covenant gave birth to bondage, and is represented by Hagar. Yes, you read that right. Jerusalem as we now know it, the centerpiece of the entire system of Law, corresponds to Hagar! (Not Sarah!) And its inhabitants, those who practice the Jewish religion, who remain in bondage, correspond to Ishmael. On the other hand, we have the covenant of the Promise given to Abraham directly. That covenant is represented by Sarah, and corresponds to the Jerusalem above. As it is written, "It's time for all the women without children to cheer up, because they're going to produce more offspring than the women who already have children." We who are free through faith in Christ are the ones who will inhabit this New Jerusalem. Indeed, we, the people of faith and not of the Law, are the ones who correspond to Isaac, for we are the children of the Promise.

Now these false teachers are troubling you just as Ishmael, the child born of human striving, harassed Isaac, the child born of the Spirit's impulse. What does the Bible say about that? "Throw out the maidservant and her son. The son of the maidservant will not be a co-heir with the son of the free woman." Well, that word is for us today. You've got to throw out the Law, and toss out the false teachers right along with it. We are not children of bondage, Church; we are children of the free woman!

5 So please hold your ground and commit to remaining in the freedom Jesus paid for, and don't be entangled by the bondage that comes with the Law. In the specific case of circumcision, I am telling you, if you go get yourself circumcised, not only will it profit you nothing, you'll also be obligated to keep the entire rest of the Law! If you try to achieve your right-standing with God by observing some facet of the Law, you'll essentially be severing all relationship between you and Jesus. Don't fall from grace that way! It's the Holy Spirit who stirs up the hope of righteousness in us, and it's Jesus who completed all the work necessary to effect that righteousness. Whether or not you're circumcised has nothing to do with it. It's all accomplished through faith, and it was only made possible by His great love.

You were doing so well. Who was it that derailed you? This perversion of the truth definitely didn't come from God. And now a tiny bit of false teaching has permeated the church like a pinch of yeast makes its way through the whole ball of dough. I am confident that, by God's grace, you will heed my words and stand up against this heresy. But the ones who are propagating this lie will face God's judgment. Anyone who says that I support the practice of circumcision is lying. If I were in favor of circumcision, then I wouldn't be a target for persecution, now would I? See, it's the idea that *the cross, all by itself, is enough to save* that makes people squirm. It offends them because it says to them that they aren't able to earn it. And they've been banking on earning it their whole lives. If I had my way, we would have these circumcision proponents just go all the way and castrate themselves!

Now, let me be clear. What I have been saying is that you are free from the requirements of the Mosaic Law. Don't think for a minute that means you are free to live any way you want! I'm not saying that at all. God still has a standard of conduct that we must adhere to. That standard has remained unchanged from the beginning. It begins and ends with loving God and loving each other, serving and showing preferential treatment to one another. God's eternal "law" is fulfilled as we obey this command.

And people who love God and love others simply DO NOT engage in egregious sinful behaviors. This is so obvious I shouldn't even have to mention it, but I know if I don't, somebody will try to take license where no license is available to take. I'm talking about things like adultery and any other type of sexual engagement outside the bonds of marriage (one man and one woman), reckless extravagance and uncurbed lust, being driven by thoughts of sex, idolatry, sorcery and witchcraft, hatred of others, engaging in contentious disputes and wrangling, jealousy and unfounded indignation, the kind of anger that boils up and explodes before composure is regained, self-promotion, seditious division, heresies and sectarianism, envy, murders, drunkenness and the riotous behavior it leads to, and so on. These sins, and others like them, come about when we refuse to allow the Holy Spirit to direct our lives and instead allow the sin factory inside us to produce its filth. I've told you before and I'm telling you again, people who live life this way WILL NOT inherit the kingdom of God!

But the fruit of holiness that the Spirit produces in us is expressed in these ways: love, joy, peace, patience, kindness, goodness, faithfulness, gentleness, and self-control. Moses' Law doesn't forbid this kind of living. In fact, no law does. But the cross of Christ *is* required in order to produce this fruit. You have to get on the cross and kill off your worldly appetites. Then God will do the work of cultivating the new you, the holy you.

So, walk in the Spirit. After all, the Spirit is your very life-source. Don't bite and devour each other like wild animals.

Don't provoke each other. Don't think too highly of yourself, and don't be jealous of others. God is not glorified by such displays of disunity and destruction.

6 Anyone in the Church who succumbs to temptation and falls into sin should be restored by the spiritual leaders, provided, of course, that the offender is actually repentant. *[I've written elsewhere about what to do with those who are unrepentant.]* It's important, though, that the ones doing the restoration do so with humility and gentleness, knowing that they're just as prone to temptation. We've got to bear each other's burdens. This is the way that we fulfill the law of Christ. Anyone who is not willing to serve someone else is deceived about his own worth and status. Don't compare yourselves to each other. When you compare yourself to someone whom you deem to be more spiritual, you give yourself a false sense of inferiority. And when you compare yourself to someone whom you deem to be less spiritual, you give yourself a false sense of superiority. Instead of comparisons, just do your best to obey the Lord and rest in the affirmation of your Father, knowing that He is in charge of making you exactly who He wants you to be, in His timing. That's the way we each do our part.

Those who are taught God's Word should financially support the ones who teach them. Don't be duped into picturing God as somebody who sits back and absorbs injustice. Whatever a man sows he will reap. So plant your seed into the good soil of the true ministers of God. As you sow seed into the Spirit, you will reap the abundant life of the Spirit. But if you sow seed into your own carnality and selfish desires, your crop will all be rotted out before harvest time even comes. Don't grow weary while you're waiting on your good seed planted in good ground to sprout and produce. Keep on doing good at every turn without giving up, and when it's time to reap, you'll have plenty to show for the effort. Every time you have the opportunity, do good to everybody, and especially to those who are in the faith.

I'm writing this with my own hand now. See how large I have to make the letters?! But I want to make sure you hear this message straight from my lips, so to speak. The ones who are trying to get you to be circumcised, they are simply pandering to the flesh—your flesh and theirs—and they are really just trying to avoid the persecution that comes when one claims the cross of Christ as the only mechanism for attaining righteousness. Even those who are circumcised aren't keeping the whole Law, and yet they want you to get circumcised just so they can brag about how influential they are. It's all so carnal. I say, God forbid that I brag about anything other than the cross of the Lord Jesus Christ, because it is only through that cross that the world has become dead to me, and I to it. Where Jesus is Lord, neither circumcision nor uncircumcision have any significance; the only thing that matters is that He makes you into a completely new creation! Peace and mercy rest on all those who follow this principle, for they are God's *true* Israel.

Brothers and sisters, I have the scars to prove I belong to the Lord, and that should count for something. So stop upsetting me with this stuff. We need to move on to bigger and better things.

I'll say goodbye for now. May the grace of our Lord Jesus Christ saturate each of your spirits. Amen.

Discussion Questions

WEEK 9: Galatians

- What is Paul's primary concern in this letter?
- If the Promise to Abraham was all we needed, what was the purpose of the Law? (Chapter 3)
- What is the metaphorical relationship between Sarah and Hagar and the two covenants (Chapter 4)? How would a 1st-century Jewish mind have processed this illustration?
- Paul spends 4½ chapters railing against "works of the Law," only to turn right around in the middle of Chapter 5 and insist that we maintain the "works" of holiness. Discuss the black-and-white distinction between the legalism that the Gospel forbids and the holiness that the Gospel requires.

EPHESIANS

1 To the holy and faithful Christians living in Ephesus,

This is Paul, an apostle of King Jesus according to God's will, wishing you grace and peace from God our Father and the Lord Jesus Christ.

Praise be to God, the Father of our Lord Jesus Christ! Through Jesus, God has poured out on us every last drop of the bounty of heaven. He picked us to be on *Team Jesus* before He even created the world. Our sport is love, our uniform is blamelessness, and our game plan is holiness. From the beginning He had in mind that a day would come when He would reveal us as His sons and fill us up with His grace. This, also, He did through Jesus. And everything He has done for us He did simply because it made Him happy. Even though we reap the benefit, His whole plan was enacted really just to bring more glory to Himself.

Everything we have is because of Him and because we are "in Him." We've been released from slavery to sin, our freedom having been purchased by His own blood. Our sins have been forgiven by the power of His abundant grace, which, in His unfathomable wisdom, He has heaped onto us. We have come to know Jesus, the incarnate Revelation of the longstanding mystery of God's rescue plan for humanity. We have found the way of faith, grasping it initially when we heard the Gospel being preached. (The Jews received the message first, and then the Gentiles heard it, too.) We have obtained an inheritance by

God's divine will and sovereignty. And we have been given the Holy Spirit, who is the Deposit guaranteeing that inheritance. When we finally claim our full inheritance in eternity, God will, with great joy, redeem His claim-ticket on us and gather us all up to be with Him forever. Then everything in heaven and on earth will be under Christ's perfect rule. Glory to God!

Ever since I heard of your faith in Jesus as Lord and your love for all the saints, I have not stopped thanking God for you. When I pray for you, I ask that God would download you with the Spirit of wisdom. I ask that He would reveal Himself to you in a fresh, eye-opening, life-changing way. I pray that you would become acutely aware that He has called you out of darkness into light, and that this sensibility would lead you to a place of unshakable confidence. He has given us an inheritance that is absolutely glorious. And He wants to display His power and authority in us and through us as our faith grows more and more. Yes, this is the very same power that He used to raise Christ from the dead, and the very same authority that He bestowed on Him when He ascended. King Jesus reigns over every colonel, sergeant, and private in Satan's army, now and forever! God has put every particle of creation under Jesus' authority. And because He has all authority, we have all authority in His name, because we are His body here on earth. We are the ones who execute His agenda. We are the ones who make up the full complement of cargo and crew for His unsinkable ship. My prayer is that God would make these truths an ongoing, tangible reality in your daily lives.

2 You were dead because of your sinful nature and the sins it produced. But God brought you to life! You were once a bunch of rebellious, good-for-nothing punks, doing everything the world says is okay, following every carnal instinct and giving in to every sinful desire, constantly tuned in to the devil's radio frequency. You were headed for the wrath of God at breakneck pace. But even when we were in that miserable, helpless state, God demonstrated His great mercy and love toward us. He raised us from death to life *with Christ*, and He seated us in the heavens *in Christ.* If you think you're blown away by His kindness right now, just imagine what it will be like in eternity when the full force of His love smacks you in the face.

You have been saved by grace through faith. That's not something you could have ever earned. It's a gift given by God alone. If we could have attained this salvation merely by keeping the Law of Moses, then it would be something we could brag about. But nobody can access it that way, and therefore, nobody has the right to brag about it. We are the handi-*work* of God. And He made us, through Jesus, in order to do good *works.* But we don't do the *work* of salvation; that's His job.

So don't lose sight of the fact that you Gentiles were once lost and hopeless, with no connection to God and no knowledge of His Son. You were not citizens of Israel, you could not reap the benefit of any of God's covenants, and you had no claim to God's Promise. They even derisively called you "uncircumcised," which was just their way of saying that you were outsiders who were not welcome in their club.

But now, you who were so far from God have been brought near to Him by means of Christ's blood. He demolished the wall that separated Jews and Gentiles. He rendered the Mosaic Law inoperative on the day when He gave His body to be shredded to death. Because He sacrificed Himself, we no longer have to make ritual sacrifices for ourselves. The result is a lasting peace, indeed an all-out unification of the two groups—Jew and Gentile—into one body, and full reconciliation of both to God through the cross. When Jesus came to earth, He spoke of delivering peace to both groups. And they both have access to the Father through the Son by only one Spirit.

Well, that means you're not strangers and foreigners anymore. You've actually become fellow citizens with God's people and members of His household. This house is being built on the foundation of the apostles and prophets, with Jesus being the primary building block from which all other stones come into alignment. Jews and Gentiles are being built up together to make this house. It's being constructed according to the most precise of specs, and when it's completed, it will be a holy temple for the Lord, the place where God's Spirit will rest comfortably.

3 It's because of this marvelous revelation—that the Gentiles have been made co-heirs with the Jews, members of one Body, and recipients of the Promise through Jesus—that God pressed me into service, giving me a special calling to preach this Good News to you Gentiles. The Holy Spirit has revealed this mystery to me, as well as to other apostles and prophets. The men and women of God in the generations before Christ could not see the whole picture. But now we have it, and I trust that as you read what I am writing, it will be revealed to you, too.

Why He picked me I still don't quite understand, since I was about as horrible a person as you can possibly be. But He did. He turned me completely around, and I am totally sold out to Him. And now He wants me to share with you this message of the limitless blessing of Christ, to make you stewards of the mystery that was hidden from previous generations. Why? So that God can use the Church to display His multifaceted wisdom to the whole of the angelic and demonic realms. In so doing, He will achieve His own purposes; the mission that was accomplished by Christ's earth-journey will bear its fruit through us! Knowing this should produce the kind of faith that will allow you to boldly lay claim to a direct-access pass to God's presence. (So, don't be discouraged just because I'm going through this difficult experience, because all the ins and outs of my odyssey have been for your benefit.)

Yes, my dear Ephesians, because God has given me the task of overseeing your discipleship, I regularly kneel before the Father, whose name is freely bestowed upon all of His children. I petition Him to give you internal fortitude through His Spirit, that your faith would grow and that you would come to know Jesus in a more tangible way. And I pray that you would really get a clear picture of the immeasurable magnitude of Christ's love. It is wider, longer, deeper, and higher than you can imagine. I pray for that love to take root in your hearts and establish the foundation of your spiritual lives. And I pray that all the fullness of God would be compressed down and stuffed into your hearts.

Oh, God, You are able to do exceedingly abundantly more than we could ask or think. And You want to use the power You've activated within *us* to do it! So, let Your Church glorify You in all that we do, now and forevermore. Amen.

4 Because God has done all of this for you, I am encouraging you in the strongest possible terms to walk worthy of the calling with which you were called. Become career professionals in humility, gentleness, and patience. Let the Holy Spirit do His work of cultivating the love of God in you to the point where you are able to overlook your neighbors' faults, keep the peace, and maintain unity. You all need to be of *one* mind and heart, because there's only one Holy Spirit, one Body of Christ, one universal calling, one hope, one Lord, one faith, one baptism, and one Father God. He's the One who sits enthroned above the earth, He's the One who works behind the scenes of every situation, and He's the One living in you!

Now, just because we're supposed to be unified doesn't mean we all have identical jobs. Each one of us has been graced to perform a certain function within the Body of Christ. This is what the Scripture was referring to when it said, "He ascended to heaven, took captives, and gave gifts to His people." (Now, when it says *ascended* it presumes a prior *descent*, which, of course, was also true of Jesus. So, He descended to earth in humility, set us free from captivity to sin, claimed us as His own captives, and then ascended. Now His presence can be felt in every corner of the cosmos.)

So, to each individual believer a gift has been given, as determined by Christ, for the benefit of the collective. But to the Church as a whole He gave the five ministerial offices: apostles, prophets, evangelists, shepherds, and teachers. These offices, and the people who hold them, have been established for the purpose of equipping the saints for the work of ministry and building up the Body of Christ just like a skyscraper is constructed from the ground up. These ministries will continue on until the Church looks exactly like Jesus, mature and complete, united in faith, knowing Him intimately, operating with the fullness of His power and love. These ministers of God raise us from spiritual childhood to spiritual adulthood. They instill in us a spiritual anchor that keeps us from drifting here and there every time the winds of newfangled doctrines blow, every time some cunning schemers try to trick and deceive us. When we are guided by this quintet of ministerial leadership God has established, we begin to grow up and become the kind of Body that is befitting a Head like King Jesus. As we each perform our specific duties, all the while encouraging each other with truth and in love, we are drawn closer and closer to each other, becoming effective as we work together in health and wholeness.

The Lord wants me to exhort you to continue moving in that direction. Don't walk in the way of the Gentiles. Their minds are still depraved and they are trying to navigate life in pitch-blackness. They are willfully ignorant, having hardened their hearts. They have become desensitized to the sting of sin on the conscience, so they practice whatever they want—greed, unbridled lust, sexual unrestraint. By going down this path, they have estranged themselves from God.

But you know better than to do those kinds of things (if you've actually come to know Him and learn from Him). You have been taught to put away all of the sinful ways you used to walk in, and to put into practice the ways of the Spirit—righteousness and holiness—walking in keeping with your new identity and allowing Him to renew your mind.

So, stop lying. "Everybody speak truthfully with your neighbor," says the Scripture. Don't allow anger to control your actions and lead you into sin. Any issues that cause you to react adversely, settle them before you go to bed at night. Don't carry that kind of negativity into the next day. It gives the devil a foothold in your life. If you used to steal, stop stealing. Instead, be diligent to find a job and do it to the best of your ability. By making a wage, you will be able to support yourself and give to those in need. Don't speak a single word that is worthless, but speak things that build people up and shower them with grace. Don't grieve the Holy Spirit; He has sealed you for the day of redemption. So put away all bitter wickedness, boiling-and-subsiding indignant anger, an angry disposition, trouble-making and bad-mouthing, and depraved ill-will toward others. Instead, be kind and compassionate toward one another, forgiving each other's sins as God forgave you through Christ.

5 Imitate God like a child picking up his father's personality traits. Exhibit the kind of love that Christ showed us, giving Himself as a sweet-smelling, sacrificial offering to God. Don't let the heinous sins of the world—sexual immorality, uncurbed lust, and greed—even be part of your conversations. Obscenities, idle chatter, and off-color joking are not suitable for the Christian either; what you should be doing is giving thanks. No fornicator, uninhibited sinner, or greedy person will inherit the Kingdom of God. They have made their choices and enthroned their idols in place of King Jesus. So, don't consort with that crowd. The wrath of God is being stored up for people who disobey God in this way. Don't let anyone talk you into thinking it isn't.

You used to be in the dark, too, but now you are God's light in this world. So be sure that you walk as children of light, searching out the perfect will of God. The hallmarks of light are goodness, righteousness, and truth. Exhibit these, and don't participate in the works of darkness. Instead, expose them. It's shameful to even talk about the things evil people do when they think nobody's looking. But the light exposes these things. Yes, the Lord is calling all those who have not yet fully surrendered to Him. Can you hear Him? "Wake up, sleepyhead! Get up, corpse! Allow Christ to shine His light on you!"

So, be careful and diligent, operating in God's abundant wisdom, doing His will, not acting foolishly. Don't waste the time God has given you. Evil is all around and increasing.

Don't get drunk. That's immoral. Instead let the infilling of the Holy Spirit be your source of pleasure. Let Him inspire you to speak life to one another through psalms and hymns and spiritual songs. Sing and make melody in your hearts to the Lord, continually giving thanks to the Father for everything in the name of the Lord Jesus Christ.

Submit to one another in the fear of God.

Wives, take a step back and allow your husbands to assume the role of knight-in-shining-armor. Do this in the same way that you cede this responsibility to Christ. For the husband is the wife's hero as Christ is the Hero and Savior of the Church, which is His body. Just as believers yield themselves to the leadership of Christ in confident assurance that He does everything in their best interest, so also should wives trust their husbands to continually act on their behalf. In so doing, the wife empowers and invigorates the husband.

Husbands, give selflessly and endlessly to your wives just as Christ gave everything of Himself for the Church, washing her clean with the water of the Word, and presenting her to Himself as a radiant bride with no trace of imperfections. In the same way husbands are to give their wives preferential treatment, putting them on a pedestal, and demonstrably ascribing worth to them through continuous servitude. He who values his wife values himself. Who ever heard of anyone neglecting to meet the needs of his own body? No, you feed it and you nurse it back to health when it's sick. That's the way Jesus cares for His Church, and that's the way a husband is to care for his wife. Just as we are Christ's very flesh and bone, so the wife is the flesh and bone of the husband, and "the man leaves his father and mother to join with his wife and become one." Mysterious, yes, but Christ is one with His Bride, and husbands should likewise be one with their wives. So, once again, every husband should love his wife just as if she's part of his own body, and every wife should give all due respect to her husband.

6 Children, obey your parents. That's doing the right thing. "Honor your father and mother" was the first commandment that came with a conditional promise: "so that life will go well and you'll live out your full allotment of time on earth."

Fathers, don't provoke your children. Always discipline them with an eye toward their future—their adulthood and their eternity—not at your own whims. Nurture them and train them in the ways of the Lord.

Employees, you need to be good witnesses for Jesus in the workplace. Do everything your boss tells you to do to the best of your ability, in a timely manner. Don't just put on a show of work ethic while the boss is watching, and then turn around and sluff off when you're left on your own. Treat that job as if you're working for God directly. You wouldn't want to give Him any less than your best, so don't do that to the people you work for. Keep in mind that God is going to reward us for what we do in His name, whether we are employees or employers.

So, employers, you, too, need to conduct your business with integrity. Don't threaten your employees or treat them unfairly. Don't forget that you have a Boss in heaven, and He treats everyone justly, irrespective of our position in society.

Finally, Church, use the power God has given you to keep yourself strong in Him. Dress yourself for battle with every piece of God's armor so that you will be fully prepared to hold your ground against the devil's tactics. We're not fighting against human beings; we're fighting against the combined armed forces of darkness—demon generals, demon colonels, demon lieutenants, and demon corporals. So put on all of God's armor so that when these evil spirits come against you, you can ably resist them. Then when the battle's over and the smoke has cleared, you'll be the one left standing, shouting, "Victory is mine through Christ!"

So, never cease to wage war against evil. Put on the belt of truth and the breastplate of righteousness, the helmet of salvation, and boots that show you're ready to go anywhere to preach the gospel of peace. Most importantly, hold up the shield of faith to block the fiery arrows the devil is shooting at you. For offense, carry the sword of the Spirit, which is God's Word. When the things you say align with the things He says, you slice through the enemy like a hot knife through butter. So, pray in the Spirit continually, being diligent to petition the Lord on behalf of yourself and others. (And pray for me, too, that, despite my chains, I might fulfill my mission as an ambassador of the Gospel, that the Word of God would be in my mouth to preach the mystery of the Gospel with boldness.)

I'm sending Tychicus to you with this letter. He'll be able to fill in all the details about what's been happening here. He is a beloved brother and a faithful minister in the Lord. I know he will be extremely encouraging to you.

Goodbye for now. Peace, love, and faith from God the Father and the Lord Jesus Christ be with you all. I declare an extra measure of grace for those who sincerely love Jesus. Amen.

Discussion Questions

WEEK 10: Ephesians

- What is the overarching thought Paul is conveying in the opening theological half of the letter (Chapters 1-3)?

- When Paul exhorts us to "walk worthy of the call" at the beginning of Chapter 4, what kinds of things is he referring to?

- Ephesians 5:22-6:9 is all written in the context of Ephesians 5:21, "Submit to one another out of reverence for Christ." (NIV) Discuss the *ways* in which the wife is to love and submit herself to the husband, and the *ways* in which the husband is to love and submit himself to the wife. What are the purposes for these different *ways* that we demonstrate our love and deference?

- How does the meaning of "stand" in the paraphrase of Ephesians 6 augment your understanding of the "armor-of-God" passage? Are we supposed to be *standing victorious* or *standing, barely*?

COLOSSIANS

1 To the holy people in Colossae who are dedicated to Christ,

This is Paul, an apostle of King Jesus by the will of God, and Timothy, your brother, wishing you grace and peace from God our Father and the Lord Jesus Christ.

What a joy it was to hear from Epaphras about your conversion! He is our fellow servant, and obviously, he has done a tremendous job ministering to you there. He told us how you had received the revelation of Jesus and had begun to trust fully in Him and show His love to all the saints. The Gospel has birthed in you the confident assurance of the eternal blessing of heaven. And you should know that this same message of hope is springing up all over the world just as it has in you!

Ever since we heard the news about you, we have not stopped praying for you. We thank God for His mercy and grace toward you. We ask Him to fill you with the knowledge of His will, and for an extra dose of His wisdom and understanding. We ask Him to empower you to live lives that are pleasing to Him, that you would bear the fruit of holiness, and that He would directly impart to you an intimate knowledge of Himself. And we ask that He would strengthen you from His storehouse of power, to be patient and able to withstand suffering while maintaining the joy of the Lord with a heart of thanksgiving toward God. For He has signed our transfer papers, and we have now been delivered out of darkness and into light. This is our rightful inheritance as His holy children. We've been purchased by the blood of Jesus, and our sins are forgiven. Now we all have reserved seats at the King's table.

Friends, I want you to really take time to soak this in. Here's what you need to understand about Jesus:

> Even though we can't see God, when we look at Jesus we are able to see and know exactly what God looks like. Seeing Jesus is like looking at the Father in the mirror, or observing the impression of the Father's seal in hot wax. When we see the Son, we know we're looking at precisely everything the Father is and nothing He's not. Jesus holds the favored position over every created thing, like a firstborn son who lays claim to the birthright and special blessing of his father. Everything that has ever been made—everything on earth and everything in heaven, everything we can see and everything we can't see, even the myriad angelic hosts (and their rebellious counterparts!)—everything has been made by Him and through Him and for Him. He stands before them all, as their unrivaled superior. It is only through Him that they can claim any semblance of form or function. He is their very origin.
>
> Furthermore, He is one with His Church as a head is one with a body. He directs us, and we, in turn, impose His will on the earth. There is no separation or disconnection between Him and us.
>
> He also holds the "firstborn" rank (in other words, the favored position or the highest status) when it comes to the resurrection of the dead. Because He conquered death, we, His brothers and sisters, will also one day rise again to meet Him and live with Him forever.
>
> Every iota of the Father's essence resides in the Son. That's why He was able to reconcile all things to Himself. It was because of the peace made possible by the blood that streamed down from His body at the cross. And this entire master plan seemed good to the Father.

Church, He has reconciled you, too! You, who once were alienated from Him because of the evil you practiced, have now been restored to right relationship with God by His tortuous death, which has made you holy and blameless in His sight. That is, provided, of course, that you continue on in the faith to the end without wavering, and you don't throw your precious hope away during trying times. (Along with everybody else, you heard this hope called *the Gospel*, of which I, Paul, am a minister. I trust you have received and believed it. Don't prove me wrong!)

I take joy in the privilege of suffering the pain and discomfort of persecution for your sakes, as did the Lord. God plunged me into this ministry, according to His wise administrative prerogative. His message, formerly a mystery to my kinsmen, is now being revealed. God is showing them that His plan is to extend His mercy to you Gentiles, too, so Christ may live in you and be your hope as well as theirs.

We preach Christ alone, and we don't pull any punches, because we want to see every man and woman reach full maturity in Him. This is the goal of all my hard labors (or, I should say, all of the work that He does *through* me).

2 I wish you could understand how I fight for you in the Spirit. Not just you, but also those in Laodicea and the other churches I've never been able to visit. I want to see you all encouraged, unified in love, and living up to the potential you have in Him to access an infinite supply of wisdom and understanding.

I'm going to say this, and I want you to listen up. If you don't hold tightly to what you were taught at the start, it won't be too difficult for folks to come in and begin to deceive you into believing a lie just because they have a way with words. I think in some cases it's already happening. So be on guard! I know I'm not there, but I am with you in spirit, and I am looking forward to hearing how you have stayed the course. So, walk in the Lord in the very same way you received Him, planted, growing up, and blossoming in the faith you were taught, thanking the Lord all the way along the journey.

Here is the warning: Don't let anyone talk you out of what you know to be true, simply because they seem to be well-versed in philosophy and history, or they claim to have insight into spiritual things, or they say they know the science behind how the world was put together. They have accumulated their knowledge the world's way, not by the revelation of Christ. They are in deception, and they are trying to deceive you.

This is the truth: 100% of God's God-ness resides in the body of the human being we call *Jesus*. He supersedes every ruler and authority, and you don't need anything other than Him in order to be complete.

It was *through Him*, not according to man's ideas and efforts, that you underwent the rites of baptism and circumcision. Your circumcision was not physical, but spiritual, a cutting away of your sins and the shackles that tied you to them. Your baptism, likewise, was a spiritual event by which you were identified with the death, burial, and resurrection of Christ. Now your old self has been killed off, and you are free to live the new life that He makes possible. This is a life of complete forgiveness, because He nailed our I.O.U. of sin and guilt to the cross. In so doing, He rendered all of the forces of evil impotent, subjecting them to public humiliation.

You've got one group of people who want to make you feel guilty just because you eat or drink something they don't think you should, or because you don't make a big to-do about the days and events they consider holy or otherwise significant. Nonsense. Those things are mere shadows of the reality that is Christ.

And then you've got another group of people that will put a guilt trip on you if you don't feign humility through extreme self-denial. Worse yet, they're trying to get you to worship angels. They say they've had visions and they've been given special insights. I'm not buying it! The only thing special about them is the inordinate amount of pride in their hearts! I dare say they're not even connected to Christ, as you, the Body, are.

So, don't let anyone talk you into receiving unwarranted

condemnation onto yourself for these things. The death your old self died with Christ was a death to the ways of the world. So there's no need to continue subjecting yourself to the world's rules: "Don't touch, don't taste, don't handle." People who enforce such rules are living in the past. They have the appearance of piety because we somehow think it looks good to prove a certain level of devotion through stoicism and asceticism. But it's all for show, and it's a currency that has no value in God's economy. Every exercise of *will power* eventually fails if the *true power* of our Lord is not behind it, because without Him, there's sin still hiding deep down in the recesses of every man and woman.

3 So, if you were buried and raised into a new life in Christ, don't pay any mind to the ways of the world. Begin to crave and search out those things that are above, where He is seated in all authority. Let me say that again: *set your minds on the things above, not on the things on earth*, because you are dead with respect to worldly life, and your new life is a mystery in God that only Jesus has the key to unlock. When He appears again, everything will be revealed, and we will get to share in His glory! Can you imagine it?!

Since you are dead to the world, make that death a reality by killing off all the parts of you that are inclined toward worldly things: all manner of sexual immorality, reckless extravagance, depraved passions, wicked intentions, unbridled lust, and the unholy desire for the possessions of others, which is really just another way of saying *idolatry*. At the appointed time, the dam that is holding back the reservoir of God's wrath will be obliterated, and the ensuing flood will overwhelm all those who rebel against Him in these ways. (And don't forget you used to be counted among them! Thank God for grace!)

So get out your scalpel and start cutting the things out of your life that shouldn't be there: an angry disposition as well as boiling-and-subsiding anger, the kind of wickedness that has no regard for the law, slander, foul language, and lying. Those behaviors have no place in the Christian walk, because we have done away with our former self, and we've received the new self that bears God's image. And that image is Christ in you; it's not your nationality, your gender, your ethnicity, your station in life, nor anything else so trivial.

I've given just a partial list of things you shouldn't be doing. Now let me tell you some things that you, as God's holy and beloved chosen people, *should* be doing. Cultivate a deep empathy and merciful compassion for people. Be kind and maintain a humble opinion of yourself. Be gentle and grow in your ability to withstand other folks' bad behavior. Help bear each other's burdens. Forgive one another. If a complaint or accusation is leveled against you, you have to forgive as Christ forgave you. Most of all, dress yourself in love, which binds us together perfectly. Let God's peace govern your actions and emotions, because everyone in the Body of Christ is called to live peaceably with everyone else. And be thankful.

The truth and conviction of the Gospel message is a living wisdom that you should allow to saturate you like a wet sponge. From your overflowing spiritual well, instruct and encourage each other, not only with spoken words, but also with songs: Scripture-songs, well-crafted songs of praise and doctrinal purity, and also your own personal songs that are birthed from the Spirit of God who lives within you. Sing these songs from your heart as a joyous response to God's grace. And whatever you say and whatever you do, do it all in the name of Jesus our Master, giving thanks to the Father through Him.

Now, let me say a few brief words about proper interpersonal relationships. Wives, step back and give your husbands the space and support they need to assume their godly role of leadership in the home. Husbands, give your all to your wives, which is the true expression of godly love. Don't let exasperation and irritability be the *modus operandi* of your marriage. Children, obey your parents in all things; this is so pleasing to the Lord. Fathers, don't stir up discouragement in your children by being short-sighted and out-of-control in the way you interact with them. The cup of your affirmation needs to sit on a level surface free from seismic activity. Don't let it spill through constant and unnecessary aggravation. Employees, do everything your employers ask of you, displaying godly fear and a good attitude, not merely an outward compliance. Whatever you do, do it with all your heart as unto the Lord, not to men, because the ultimate reward will come from Him, not in this life, but when we receive our inheritance as His sons. Don't forget, your real Boss is the Messiah. He's the One you're really serving. (Of course, on the other hand, those who practice wrongdoing will get their reward, too. God is 100% just when it comes to these things.) **4** Employers, treat your employees well, and make sure you pay them appropriately. Remember, you've got a Boss, too, and He's watching you.

Continue to pray with disciplined regularity and gratitude. In particular continue praying for us, that God would open every door He sees fit to open, giving us opportunities to share the mystery of Christ, for whom I am in chains; and that we would have the wherewithal to walk through those open doors, speaking with clarity everything He wants said. Be wise in your interactions with those outside the faith, making the most of every opportunity. Speak gently and lovingly without sacrificing the truth. The flavor of the message can be contextualized, but don't remove its nutritional content. God will give you the wisdom to know how to influence each person.

I'm sending Tychicus to you to fill you in on the details of my recent activities. He has been faithful to the Lord, serving Him and ministering to His people well. We love him so much, and I know he will be a great encouragement to you. As will Onesimus. He's one of your own, and he, too, will be able to communicate what's been happening here.

Aristarchus, who is with me here in prison, sends his greetings, as does Jesus (the Jesus we call *Justus*), as well as Barnabus' cousin, Mark. (Barnabus was the one I sent you instructions about. Please be sure to welcome him if he's able to come see you.) These guys are the only ones in my current crew who are Jewish by birth. They have been an indispensable encouragement to me as we work together for the kingdom's sake.

Our beloved doctor, Luke, says, "Hello," too. As does Demas. Epaphras also sends greetings. He is a slave of Christ, and, take my word for it, he works tirelessly in petitioning the Lord for you to find wholeness in God's perfect will. (He does the same thing for the churches in the two towns just north of you, too.) Speaking of which, please say "Hi" to the folks in Laodicea for me, and be sure to give my greetings to Nympha and the church that meets in her house. And tell Archippus I said to be sure he completes the ministry the Lord gave him. After you read this letter, send it on to the Laodicean church so they can read it, too. And get the letter I wrote to them so you can read that one.

This is me, Paul, signing off in my own handwriting. Don't forget to bring me up before the Lord, reminding Him of my imprisonment, and asking Him for His continued grace. And may His grace be with you, too. Amen.

Discussion Questions

WEEK 11: Colossians

- According to Chapter 1, who is Jesus and what is it that He does for us?
- How does Paul's articulation of Christology in Chapter 1 tie in to his concerns for the Colossians in Chapter 2?
- Colossians 3:2 echoes Romans 8:5. Discuss the importance of "setting our minds" on the things above. Come up with some practical ways that you can actually succeed in "setting your mind" throughout your daily life.
- As is Paul's tendency, he shifts from more of a theological focus to more of a practical focus in the back half of the letter. Discuss some of the ways he directs us to walk the walk.

PAUL'S LETTER TO THE

PHILIPPIANS

1 Dear saints of Philippi—bishops and deacons and all who are
in Christ Jesus,

May the fullness of grace and peace from God our Father and
the Lord Jesus Christ be yours.

I give God thanks every time you come to mind, which is all
the time. Virtually every time I pray I joyously petition the Lord
on your behalf. You have never wavered in your dedication to
the Gospel, and to me, since the day you were converted. And I
know that the One who charted your new course in the Spirit
will see it through to completion on the day Jesus returns. It's
right for me to think this way about you, because I know you are
cut from the same cloth I am when it comes to defending and
confirming the Gospel, even to the point of imprisonment. And
I know you're all enjoying the same grace I am, too. God is my
witness, I mean it when I say that the Lord has put a real soft
spot in my heart for you.

So, this is what I pray for you: that God's love will
overwhelm you as you begin to know Him more and discern His
thoughts and ways, distinguishing what's merely *good* from what
is *God*; that you would be pure and free from offense until the
Lord returns; and that you would be filled with the fruits of
righteousness, which are only produced by Christ Jesus to the
glory and praise of God.

Now Church, you should know that the trials and setbacks
I've had have actually served to advance the Gospel. Even the

palace guard here in Rome has come to recognize that it's because of Christ that I am in chains. And my imprisonment has invigorated most of the Christians around here, who are now proclaiming the Word boldly and fearlessly.

Yes, there are some who preach Christ from impure motives, being jealous, striving, etc. But others do preach with pure motives. The impure preachers are selfish and just trying to make a name for themselves; they don't care that they're hurting me that much more. The pure preachers minister out of God's love, and they support me because they know I have been directly appointed by God and I am a defender of the true Gospel. The bottom line is: whether Christ is preached from pure motives or from impure motives, I am just excited that the message about Him is being preached. God can use all of it for good.

Indeed, I maintain my joy and encouragement because I know that one day, due in part to your prayers, I will be vindicated by the Spirit of Jesus Christ. There may be some who are ashamed of me because of the situation I'm in, but I am of a constitution never to be ashamed about anything, knowing that my King is receiving honor through every challenge I meet with courage—whether a trial of life or even the trial of death.

See, this is how I think about it: if I'm alive, it's not actually my life being lived out, it's Christ living His life through me. So, I won't be losing anything when I die. Death would be a great gain to me. On the one hand, I can see the benefit of living on for some time to come. I would be able to do more kingdom work in that case. It would be more beneficial to you for me to continue to work on this earth on your behalf, and I would be happy to have that opportunity. On the other hand, I do long to move on and meet the Lord face to face, which would be way better for me! So, I go back and forth in my own mind as to which one I want, and which one the Lord wants. For now, I'm convinced I'll live at least a bit longer, so that I'll be able to help you grow in joy and faith. And if I get to see you again, you'll be able to heap praises onto Him because of what He's done.

Whether or not I get to come see you, make sure you are living life in a manner worthy of the Gospel of Christ, day in and day out. Even if I'm not there physically, I will certainly hear how well you're doing, and I'll know that we are simpatico in our efforts on behalf of the Gospel and the Kingdom. Don't cower in the face of those who are persecuting you. You are now going through the same struggle you've seen me go through (and that I continue to go through). Know that your endurance is the sign of your salvation, and of their destruction. Be encouraged! The Lord has given you the great honor of believing in Him to the point of suffering persecution for His sake!

2 So, if you really are representative of the Church at its best, as I believe you are; if you are able to derive encouragement from Christ, your ultimate Source; if you are able to find comfort in His love; if you are able to build each other up through close relationships formed in the Spirit; if you really are tender and merciful; then top off my cup of joy by putting into practice these pinnacle attributes of true Christianity: *unity* and *humility*.

Unity meaning you have one mind. Not that you think the same way, but that your thoughts are focused on the same thing, which is Him. You should be of *His* mind. *Unity* also meaning everyone expressing the same love of God. And be good teammates, cheering each other on, each being the others' biggest fan.

Humility meaning nothing is ever done from selfish ambition, or egotism, or one-upmanship, or pomp, or self-promotion, or pride over your abilities and achievements. Instead, place a higher value on others than you place on yourself. Don't just look after your own interests, but look after the interests of others, too. Being humble means adopting the same attitude Jesus had when He came to earth:

> We're talking about One who is fully divine! All of God's essence is intrinsic to Him. (We know this

because He never gave any indication that it would be heretical to consider Himself equal to God, though He had ample opportunity to do so.)

Even so, He agreed to put His divinity in His back pocket, so to speak, choosing to accept His lot as a slave, becoming a man. Having come to grips with His newfound humanity, He *humbled* Himself by obeying God at every turn, even going so far as to die on the cross!

Because He went all the way in fulfilling the Father's will, God has highly exalted Him and given Him a name that carries an authority greater than any other name. Every knee will bow at the name of Jesus—the ones who choose to bow now, and the ones who will be forced to bow later. And every tongue will confess that Jesus is both Christ and Lord, the King of kings and the Master over all. That will be the day of God's glorious final triumph!

Friends, when I was with you, you always did everything I instructed you to do. And now that we're apart, it's that much more important that you continue to do the same. Be diligent to perform the works that evidence your salvation, posturing yourself before God with holy fear and trembling. You know that it is God who is actually doing the work in you for His own pleasure. So be yielded to Him in every area so that your growth can be exponential.

Do what's right, everything you know to do, without holding on to any secret discontent about it. Don't complain incessantly about it. And don't deliberate on it until doubt creeps in and you end up talking yourself out of doing it. In this way you will be without blame or guile, children of God placed in the middle of a perverted world of opposition, to shine as bright lights in the darkness. So, hold onto the Word, who is your source of life. That way when the King returns I can know that I haven't done all this work in vain, and I can rejoice.

Even if I end up being martyred soon, I'll rejoice in that, too. I will gladly give my life as a drink offering, pouring it right on top of your sacrifice of daily service. So, you rejoice the same way I am rejoicing, okay?

I trust that the Lord will open the door for me to send Timothy to you soon so that I can get a report of your progress and be encouraged. Nobody cares more about you than Timothy does. Everyone's tendency is to look out for self-interests, not what interests King Jesus. But you know that Timothy's character has been proven, having shadowed me for years in ministry as a son with a father. So, I hope to send him as soon as they decide what they're going to do with me. Of course, I'm trusting that the Lord will allow me to come see you soon, too.

This time, however, I thought it was the right thing to do to send Epaphroditus back to you. He is my brother, a co-worker, a co-soldier in the cause. You chose him to be the one to bring me what I needed. And he has been wanting to reunite with you, because he found out you heard he was sick, and he was distressed at the thought of you worrying over him. Indeed, he was very sick. In fact, he almost died. But God had mercy on him, and, by extension, He had mercy on me by not allowing one more sorrow to pile up on top of my many sorrows. So, I'm excited to be able to send him to you, to give you something else to rejoice about. And I'll have even less sorrow then. Cheerfully take him in and show him the honor due him in the Lord, for he has served the King well in spite of a near-death trial, fulfilling his duty in being the emissary of your ministry to me.

3 I know I'm repeating myself, but let me say it again: from now on, be sure to continue rejoicing in the Lord. Whether facing external persecution from the sworn enemies of Christ, or standing up against internal strife caused by those fake Christians who attempt to add poisonous requirements to the pure faith, know that your stance for truth is a cause for joy!

It's not a bother for me to bring this up again, but it's important for you; it's my way of keeping you safe. You *must* diligently guard against these dirty dogs, these evil people who are preaching circumcision as a necessary addition to the Gospel. For you that would be a mutilation, not only of your flesh, but also your spirits. It is *not* necessary for a follower of Christ to be circumcised. In fact, *we* are the ones whom God counts as His true people of circumcision; we who believe in Jesus Christ, whose worship of God is made perfect in Him by the Spirit, and who therefore put no stock in a mere mark upon our flesh.

Now, if there's anybody who could claim the works of Judaism as his basis for salvation, it would be me. I'm a direct descendant of Israel, from the tribe of Benjamin. I was circumcised eight days after I was born, as is the custom. I was a Pharisee, trained in the Law, which I followed to a T. And I was zealous in enforcing the Law, proving myself by spearheading the heinous persecution of the Church.

But none of that helps me now! I got ahead in man's eyes living that way, but it actually put me deeper in debt to God. I don't consider my former, Law-driven life to have made me *any* brownie points with God! Quite to the contrary, my past "achievements" mean nothing more to me than the foul stench of raw sewage. I have gladly given it all up in order to receive that which is infinitely superior: the mercy of the King, the ability to know Him, the privilege of following Him, His protection, His righteousness imputed by faith, His resurrection power at work in me, the honor of suffering as He did, the precious affiliation with His death, and the promise of resurrection for which He blazed the trail.

I'm not saying that I've arrived. I'm not perfect yet. But I press on so that I can seize that thing for which Jesus seized me. I haven't yet grasped it, but what I do is to forget everything in my past and continue reaching forward to what lies ahead, keeping my sight set on the finish line, so that I may obtain the prize that awaits us in heaven, where God has called us through Christ Jesus. As many as are mature enough to get what I'm saying here, have the same mindset I have in this. For those who just aren't there yet, God will help you to understand what I'm talking about as you grow in Him. However far each one has come, let him walk to the best of his ability according to the degree of understanding he has attained in the Lord. The important thing is that our minds are all focused in the same direction.

Brothers and sisters, follow my example, and take notice of others who walk the same way I do, so that you can follow their examples, too. I've told you horror stories before of many who have started this race only to falter along the way and turn back. They have literally become enemies of the cross of Christ. Their minds are set on earthly things, their god is their belly, they derive glory from the very things that should cause them to feel shame. Even now I have tears in my eyes as I think about them, because the truth is, they are headed for hell.

But we're not going to become rebelliously self-serving like they have, right?! We are citizens of heaven, and we are eagerly awaiting our Savior, the Lord Jesus Christ, who will descend from heaven and turn our weak and mortal bodies into glorified super-bodies. When He comes, He'll demonstrate His infinite power by subjecting everything to His own perfect kingship. **4** So, my dear Philippians, you, the church that has become my greatest legacy and has given me the greatest joy, listen to me, friends: *stand firm in the Lord!*

Euodia and Syntyche, I'm imploring both of you: settle your differences and be totally unified. Your minds have to be set on the Lord, not on your own opinions and offenses. Syzygos, I am trusting you to arbitrate this thing. You truly are a comrade-in-arms, just as your name indicates. These ladies have labored with me for the sake of the Gospel, along with Clement and several others. They are all true believers who I know have a place reserved in heaven. That's why I know they will be able to achieve peace, with the Lord's help.

What I said before is directly applicable to this situation. Rejoice in the Lord! Continually! Let me say it one more time. Rejoice! Allow a spirit of gentleness to flow through you, such that everyone recognizes it. Don't forget that Jesus is coming back soon; we don't need any distractions. So don't be anxious! No exceptions! Instead, pray about everything, bringing your requests before God, thanking Him in advance. And the peace of God, which is beyond all human comprehension, will guard your hearts and minds through Christ Jesus.

Finally, brothers and sisters, focus all of your attention on things that are true, honorable, righteous, pure, pleasing to the Lord, and from a spirit of kindness and goodwill. If something possesses moral potency or is praiseworthy, that's the kind of thing you should meditate on. Everything you learned from me and watched me put into practice, do those things. Then the God of peace will be with you.

Speaking of rejoicing in the Lord, it was I who rejoiced when I realized that you were still concerned about me. I know you haven't always had the opportunity to demonstrate your concern, but now you have, and I appreciate it so much. I'm not saying this to manipulate more support from you. Actually, I have everything I need right now, having received from Epaphroditus the gifts you sent, which are a sweet-smelling sacrifice that pleases God. I have learned how to be content regardless of my situation. I've had lean seasons and seasons of abundance. I've been full, and I've been hungry. I can handle any variety of circumstance because of the strength Christ gives me. Regardless, it's good that you saw fit to share in my suffering by sacrificing on my behalf. You and I both know that you were the only church that contributed to my mission when I took off from Macedonia. And then you twice sent me even more when I was in Thessalonica. So, I'm not looking for more funding; I'm commending you, because God is making deposits in your spiritual account for this. Yes, God will meet every one of your needs out of his infinite storehouse of blessing through Christ Jesus. To Father God be all glory. Amen.

Please say "Hello" to all the saints there for me. I send blessings in the name of Jesus Christ. All of God's people here say "Hi," too, in particular those who belong to Caesar's household.

May the grace of the Lord Jesus Christ be with each and every one of you.

Yours in love,
Paul, along with Timothy, slaves of Jesus Christ

Discussion Questions

WEEK 12: Philippians

- What problem is this church encountering, according to the last paragraph of Chapter 1?
- Discuss the extreme nature of Jesus' humbling experience, laid out in Chapter 2.
- List all of the reasons for being anxious that Paul accepts as legitimate in Chapter 4. What remedy does he give for anxiety? Discuss the ways in which this is applicable to your life.
- How does Paul's ability to be content in all circumstances compare to your outlook on life?

PAUL'S **FIRST** LETTER TO THE
CORINTHIANS

1 To the Church of God in Corinth—those who are called to holiness and are being made holy as they submit to the rulership of King Jesus.

This is Paul, a man God chose to be an apostle of Jesus, the Anointed One; and Sosthenes, our brother in the faith. We know that you call on the Lord all the time, and He is your Master, as He is ours. We send warm greetings of grace and peace from God our Father and the Lord Jesus Christ.

I thank God constantly for pouring out His grace on you through Jesus our King. Having heard the message about Him, and having come to know Him, you have become spiritually wealthy through Him. His testimony has become your testimony. You're not lacking any of His gifts. And you are eagerly awaiting His triumphant return, as well you should be. He has established you, and He will sustain you until the end, presenting you blameless before the throne of judgment on the last Day. God is faithful. He called you into fellowship with His Son, the Lord Jesus Christ, and He will fulfill that calling in you.

Now guys, I'm begging you, for Jesus' sake, talk *to* each other and *about* each other with a unified message. Don't let anything come between you, and be in perfect unity in the way you think and make daily decisions. The reason I'm bringing this up is that the folks from Chloe's house church told me that you're quarrelling about the most inconsequential of topics. Some of you are claiming to follow Paul, others Apollos, some

Peter, and others Christ. Does the King have a divided
kingdom? Was Paul the one who was crucified for you? Or were
you baptized in Paul's name? No! In fact, now I'm really glad I
didn't baptize any of you—except Crispus and Gaius—that way
you can't get the idea that the significance of baptism had
anything to do with me. (Actually, now that I'm thinking about
it, I also baptized everyone in Stephanus' family. But other than
them, I can't think of anyone else there I baptized.) See, being a
baptizer is not my primary calling. My primary calling is
preaching the Gospel, and even my preaching is uncomplicated.
I don't try to impress people with fancy words and one-liners. I
only want them to be impressed by the cross of Christ, because
all power rests in it!

Now the message of the cross is crazy-talk to those who are
headed for death, but it's the only source of God's power for us
who are walking the path to salvation. The Scripture says it this
way: "I will render the wisdom of the wise useless, and I'll make
smart people look like they know nothing." For the experts and
the scholars and all those who are so great at debating the finer
points, what possible response could they have to God's
wisdom? His simple yet profound act of righteousness has made
them all look like hamsters on a running wheel. God, in His
infinite wisdom, saw to it that nobody could ever discover Him
through natural wisdom, but instead, people can only come to
Him by humbling themselves and believing in His foolishly
simple Way. The Jews use miraculous signs as the basis of
forming new beliefs, and the Greeks base their beliefs on logic
and philosophical depth. But we preach Christ crucified and
resurrected, which, although both a miraculous sign and
eminently logical, has nevertheless, ironically, tripped up the
Jews and outwitted the Greeks. Yet to those who are called of
God, whether Jews or Greeks, Jesus Christ is the sole agent of
God's power and wisdom. God's foolishness is wiser than any
man, and God's weakness is stronger than any man.

Think about your own calling, friends. You weren't exactly
sages and brainiacs in the world's eyes when Jesus found you.

No, the wise and the powerful and the highfalutin types aren't normally the ones God chooses. He uses simplicity to shame the wise, He uses weakness to shame the powerful, and He uses the worthless to shame the valuable. Why? So that nobody can stand before Him and legitimately take credit for his own enlightenment. On the contrary, it was by His own doing that He put you into Christ Jesus, who actually becomes the wisdom of God to us—not to mention becoming our righteousness, sanctification, and redemption! That's why the Scripture says, "Anyone who brags should brag on God alone."

2 Brothers and sisters, when I first came to you, I didn't try to wax eloquent. I just laid out the Gospel plain and simple. I was determined not to present any special insight beyond the straightforward message of the crucifixion and resurrection of Jesus Christ. With weakness and fear and trembling I preached to you, not with human wisdom and persuasive rhetoric, but with a clear demonstration of the power of the Spirit. I wanted to make sure your faith was in the power of God and not the wisdom of men.

All that being said, make no mistake, we *do* have wisdom—real wisdom, the wisdom of God, not the cheap imitation of man. The wisdom we possess is a mystery that God hid from mankind in eternity past. Only those who approach Him in humility does He allow to find it and receive joy from it. The rulers of our time have proven they don't have this wisdom, because if they did, they never would have crucified the Lord of Glory. It is written, "Nobody has ever seen or heard or perceived in his heart the wonderful things God has prepared for those who love Him." But we've been given a glimpse of these things by God through His Spirit. Just like you're the only one who knows what you're thinking, the Spirit of God is the only One who knows what He's thinking. God gave us His Spirit, not the world's spirit, so that we could perceive the things He has freely given us. We talk about these things using the vocabulary of the Spirit, teaching spiritual things to spiritual people. Unspiritual people think all of this is nonsense. They can't receive this truth because they can only understand the information their natural senses give them, whereas God's wisdom must be spiritually discerned. Those who have the Holy Spirit are able to conduct a forensic investigation into spiritual realities, but those who are unspiritual do not have the tools to be able to conduct this kind of spiritual investigation. They really can't say anything meaningful about spiritual people at all because they just don't get it. They're the ones the Bible refers to when it says, "Who knows the Lord's thoughts, or who could possibly teach Him anything?" But we have actually been given the faculty to think and perceive the way Christ does.

3 Nevertheless, when I was there with you, I couldn't talk to you as if you had this spiritual faculty. I had to talk to you as if you had no such faculty, or, at least, an underdeveloped one. You were gloriously born again, but at that point you were still spiritual infants. I had to feed you with milk because you couldn't digest solid food. It's a joy to care for newborns like that, but the problem now is you're *still* not able to receive solid spiritual food. Not only are you still immature in the faith, you're even carnal, still acting on your natural, fleshly impulses, and not walking according to the impulse of the Spirit. What other possible analysis is there? You're operating in jealousy and opposition and antagonism. That's carnality. When you say, "I'm with Paul," or, "I'm with Apollos," that's your flesh talking.

Who are Paul and Apollos other than mere servants whom the Lord used as He willed to bring you to faith? We are God's workers, but you are His field. I planted, and Apollos watered, but it's God alone who produces the miracle of ripe fruit. Anybody can plant and water, but nobody can force the crops to grow. We have to give all the credit to God for that. The one who plants and the one who waters are on the same team. God is going to reward us handsomely for our work. Trust me, we don't need your fake accolades and cult followings.

Let me use another analogy: you are God's *building*. He graciously contracted me to lay the foundation of His building, and He is contracting others to build on top of that foundation.

But there's no doubt He is the owner and project manager of the building.

Now, the foundation I laid was nothing more than Jesus Christ Himself, and the other builders that come along had better be careful not to alter that foundation or build on any other. Different builders will build differently, and they will use different materials. Some will use gold and silver and precious gems, but others will use wood and hay and straw. When the fire comes, it will test the craftsmanship with which the Church has been built. Some builders' work will still be standing strong, and God will reward them. Other builders will find their work has been reduced to ashes. They will mourn their losses, but their own trial-by-fire will lead to their personal salvation.

Church, you are the new-and-improved Temple of God, and His Spirit dwells in you. That's why it's critical that His Temple remain holy. God will destroy everyone who dares to defile it.

Don't deceive yourselves. If you're one of these who seems wise according to the world's standards, throw that wisdom away and be a fool in the world's eyes so that you can gain true wisdom. The world's wisdom is foolishness to God, as it is written, "He entraps the wise by their own cunning schemes," and, "The Lord knows that every thought of the so-called wise man is futile."

You have no reason to take pride in your allegiance to a particular leader. That leader hasn't given you anything; everything has been given to you by Christ. He gave you Paul, and He gave you Apollos and Peter. He has given you the world, and He has given you life and death. He has given you things for today, and He has given you a glorious future. You don't belong to an apostle; everything belongs to you, because you belong to Christ, and Christ belongs to God.

4 So, think of us apostles as mere servants of Christ whose duty it is to unravel the mysteries of God before your eyes. Now to serve God in this way requires faithfulness on our part, and I pray we are proving faithful. Whether I'm judged faithful by you or in a court room doesn't matter much to me. I don't even bother rating myself anymore. I don't know of anything I'm doing wrong, but that's not the true basis of my innocence. Only the Lord knows the score. So don't make the mistake of ranking the apostles, or anyone else for that matter. The Lord will do that when He comes. He will expose all hidden darkness and impure motives, and every pure motive will receive His personal commendation.

Now friends, I've been using Apollos and myself as examples of how to remain humble and not presume too much of yourselves or the leaders that you're enamored with. Don't display an irreverent attitude toward God's Word by choosing the discord of these cliques over the unity of the brotherhood. Think about it, how major are these differences anyway? Not very. And did you earn your own salvation? No, it was freely given to you. And if you did receive it, why are you acting like you're not actually saved, by engaging in this prideful behavior of divisiveness?

You're acting like you've already reached the finish line, like you're so spiritually full and rich that you don't need any more sustenance and provision, like you've already claimed your crown. But you've left us behind, haven't you? Part of me wishes you were reigning on high already, because we would be reigning with you. But we're anything but reigning. I rather think God has decided to make a spectacle of us in front of the world, like the prisoners of war you would see bringing up the rear of a victory parade. Men and angels alike have seen that we are condemned to death. We are fools for Christ's sake; do you really think you're wise in Him? We are physically weak because of our devotion to Christ; do you really think you're strong in Him? We are disgraced in His service; do you really think you're distinguished in Him? So much of the time, and even still now, Apollos and I are homeless, hungry and thirsty, wearing worn-out clothes, and even getting beaten. We work hard manual labor. We are considered the lowest, most worthless garbage of the world. But when we are cursed, we still speak love and peace. When we are beaten, we still demonstrate patience and meekness. When we are slandered, we make our defense in gentleness and kindness.

I'm not writing these things to make you feel bad about yourselves, but rather as my beloved children I am warning you. Hypothetically you could have 10,000 guardians in Christ, but you don't have many fathers in the faith. I am the one who became your father through the Gospel. So I'm urging you to imitate me. This is why I sent Timothy to you. He is a faithful son in the Lord, and I love him dearly. He has been my right hand man, and he knows everything I've been teaching in every church I've visited. I trust him implicitly to remind you of my ways in Christ.

Some of you are getting too big for your britches. You assume I'm never coming back, so you're starting to talk a big game, thinking you won't have to answer for anything anymore. Well, I am coming back, and soon, if the Lord wills. And when I get there, I'll be able to tell immediately if you are all talk or if you actually have the power. See God's kingdom is about power, not words. So it's your choice: I can come with a hug and a smile, or I can come with a whoopin' stick.

5 I'm hearing reports that you are allowing sexual immorality to go unchecked. And I'm not just talking about merely inappropriate, I'm talking about full-on wickedness. You've got a guy in your church who is sleeping with his father's wife?! Are you kidding me?! We rarely even hear about that kind of gross misconduct from the world! But you're not even grieved by it. You're so prideful, you don't even realize this is a major issue. You should be mourning the fact that you're going to have to kick this guy out of the church.

I know I'm not there, but I can assure you I have already made a firm judgment on this matter. So the next time you get together, consider me to be with you in spirit, and turn this man over to Satan in the name and in the power of the Lord Jesus Christ. The purpose of such an excommunication is twofold. First, it keeps the church from becoming poisoned by this kind of influence. And second, it gives this man the opportunity to run his sinful course to its end where he wakes up one day and realizes his wicked state, repents and begs for mercy, and is saved in the Day of our Lord Jesus.

The way you're boasting about this situation is not good. Don't you know that the smallest amount of yeast permeates the whole ball of dough? Toss out this old yeast, so that you can be a new and pure ball of dough. Remember, you are unleavened, because you are the Body of Christ, and Christ was unleavened. He was the Passover Lamb who was sacrificed for us; and His body, which was broken for us, was the unleavened bread of the Passover, untainted by sin. That's why we observe the feast with unleavened bread, and that's why we live unleavened lives, practicing sincerity and truth, not malice and evil.

I already wrote a letter to you explaining how you should not hang out with sexually immoral people. But what I meant by that was that you should not fellowship with people who claim to be Christians who are yet sexually immoral. Obviously I did not mean for you to refrain from associating with the sexually immoral people of the world, because that would mean you would have to lose contact with the entire planet. We don't develop intimate relationships with greedy, conniving, idolatrous people, but we do at least interact with them; after all, they're the very ones who need the Gospel. But anyone who claims to be a Christian brother or sister who is sexually immoral, or covetous, or idolatrous, or abusive, or a drunkard, or a financial predator—don't even eat with such a person. Look, even I don't have the authority to judge those who are not part of the Church; only God does. But you and I both have the authority to judge those who claim to be the Church. So, "throw out that evil scoundrel!"

6 Here's another thing. If two of you are engaged in a dispute, why would you even think of going before the world's court system to settle it? We have a perfectly sound process for that within the Church. Don't you think Christian brothers and sisters would make a more trustworthy judge and jury than the world? The holy people of God will actually judge the world!

Don't you know that we will even judge angels? How much more so do we have the tools to be able to judge fairly in this life? Why would you take your dispute before the type of people that the Church does not regard as reputable? Is there not a single wise man among you who would make a godly judge? That's shameful. Brothers should not be bringing other brothers in front of unbelievers for judgment. You are failing miserably on this point. Why wouldn't you rather just suffer the injustice or be cheated rather than resorting to such means? But no, you're the ones doing the cheating and the wronging, and you're doing it to your own Family members.

Don't you know that unrighteous people will not inherit God's kingdom? Don't kid yourself. No manner of sexually immoral person will inherit the kingdom of God—not those who engage in sexual activity before marriage, not those who violate their marriages by sleeping with others, not the effeminate teenage boys who willingly submit themselves to men for their sexual gratification, not lesbians and not homosexual men. Neither will idolaters, thieves, the covetous, drunkards, verbal abusers, nor financial predators inherit God's kingdom. Some of you used to do these very things, but praise God, you were washed in the blood of Jesus, given a not-guilty verdict, and made holy by the Spirit of God.

Even certain things that are legal aren't necessarily things we should be doing. And for sure you shouldn't become enslaved to any of your desires, and then claim "freedom in Christ" as your excuse. If this is true for things that are fair game, such as all the things we're allowed to eat, how much more is it true for things that are off limits, such as sexual sin?! Your body was not made to indulge in shameless acts. It was made to worship God! The God who raised Christ from the dead will resurrect you one day because your bodies are members of His Body! So how could you even think of joining yourself to another—remember that's what happens when you sleep with someone; "the two" of you "become one flesh!" Would you really be so brazen as to bring a prostitute into the marriage bed with Christ and His Bride?! If you're joined to the Lord, you are one with Him in the Spirit. You can't unite with anyone else!

So run away from sexual immorality as fast and as far as you can. All the other sins one commits are outside the body, but sexual immorality is a sin committed against your own body. Don't you know that your bodies are Temples of the Holy Spirit who lives in you, whom God gave to you? You don't own yourself. You are God's slaves who were bought at a price. So honor God with your bodies.

7 Now let me get to the questions you asked in your last letter. If you're single, or a young widow, and you are able to remain celibate, go right ahead. There's a part of me that wishes everyone could be single like I am. You would certainly be able to devote more time to the kingdom that way. But everyone has different gifts from God, and I understand that for some of you, celibacy is not one of them. So, if you desire to have a spouse and a family, there's nothing wrong with that. It should certainly curb any desire to commit sexual immorality, which is *not* an option. It's better to marry than to burn with passion.

In a marriage, the husband should do everything he can to please the wife, and the wife should do everything she can to please the husband. The husband is not in charge of his own body, the wife is. And the wife is not in charge of her own body, the husband is. So don't deprive each other of your rights to each other's bodies. Now, occasionally, it would be a good idea to agree together to abstain from sexual relations for a time while you devote yourselves to prayer and fasting, before coming together again. That way you can avoid Satan's temptations. (I'm just offering this as a tip on how to stay pure. It's certainly not something you have to do.)

Married couples, I insist—actually, the Lord commands it— a wife is not to leave her husband. And if she does leave, she needs to remain unmarried, or else reconcile with her husband. And likewise, a husband is not to divorce his wife.

Now, going a bit further, this is what I would say—I won't go so far as to say it's the Lord talking—if a man who is a believer has a wife who is an unbeliever, but she is willing to stay with him, he should not divorce her; and if a woman who is a believer has a husband who is an unbeliever, but he is willing to stay with her, she should not divorce him. See, the believing spouse brings a covering of holiness over the unbelieving spouse. If not for this your children would be unholy, but because of the believing spouse, the children are holy.

On the other hand, if the unbelieving spouse wants to leave, let him or her leave. There are no further requirements for the Christian spouse at that point. He or she is totally free and at peace with God. After all, you don't know if you're going to ever lead that spouse to the Lord or not.

Now regarding your question about the young women who are unmarried, I don't have a direct Word from the Lord, but He has granted me wisdom, and He trusts me to speak into these things. Given the current situation there, I would recommend that a man stay single if he's single, and obviously, stay married if he's married. Getting married is no sin, not for the young men, and neither for the young women. However, marriage brings on some complications that I am trying to spare you from. Folks, the time is getting short. We need to be focused on the things above now more than ever. Those who are married should be as focused as if they were unmarried. Those who are sad should be so focused on what matters that they have no reason to be sad. Those who are happy in life should become so focused on what matters that any worldly pleasures that give them happiness begin to pale in comparison. Buy and sell with the understanding that your material goods are God's blessings, not your prized possessions. Interact with the world and use its resources as God intends you to: to live, to enjoy the life He's given you, and to advance His kingdom. Don't be sucked in by the trappings of the world to your own derailment. The world as we know it will soon pass away.

I want you to be able to devote your time and energy to the Lord, but a man who is married must devote his time and energy to his wife, and a woman who is married must devote her time and energy to her husband. Unmarried men and women are able to devote all of themselves to the Lord, pursuing holiness in body and spirit. I'm saying all of this for your own benefit. I'm certainly not trying to tie you down one way or another, but I would like to see everyone serve the Lord with as few distractions as possible.

However, if a young couple is beginning to think and act too passionately toward each other, as long as they are of the appropriate age, let them marry. It's not a sin. And for those who are able to keep themselves disciplined and pure without getting married, better yet. Married and committed, no problem; single and chaste, even better.

Now, those who are married must stay in that marriage, but if one spouse dies, the other is free to remarry. However, I would recommend that the widow or widower remain unmarried, for the reasons I articulated above. I think I am giving you the Spirit's guidance on this.

This advice about staying as you are when you become a Christian—single if single and married if married—applies to other areas as well. For example, one who is circumcised when he becomes a Christian should not try to become uncircumcised, and one who is uncircumcised should not get circumcised. Whether one is circumcised has no bearing on one's ability to be a good Christian. Being a Christian is about keeping God's commandments. Likewise, if you're a slave when you become a Christian, there is no issue in remaining a slave. If you are able to gain your freedom, that's wonderful. Use that freedom for His purposes. A slave who is called into Christianity is free in Him, and a free man who is called into Christianity becomes His slave. You were all purchased by God to become His slaves, so don't become enslaved to the world and its ways.

8 Now to your question about meat that comes from animals sacrificed to pagan gods. You all have different levels of understanding on this, but let's not allow what we know about a particular issue to become a source of pride for us. Just because we know something, doesn't exempt us from showing love to those who don't. A good rule of thumb is, if you think you know something, act as if you don't know anything as well as you should. Those who love God are known by Him; that's the only *knowing* that really matters.

Some of you have come to realize, correctly, that eating this meat is not a sin. There are many so-called gods in the sky and on the earth, and every single one is worthless. We know that there is only one true God, the Father from whom all things were made, and one Lord Jesus Christ, the Son through whom all things were made and through whom we live.

But there are some who believe that eating this meat *is* a sin. They are troubled by the fact that it's a byproduct of idol worship. So, when they eat the meat, they're actually violating their consciences, which is a sin *to them*. (Of course, the fact is, what we eat gets us no closer to God. Neither does not eating. But these brothers and sisters haven't come to understand that yet.) So, when you more or less force the issue on them, you're doing them harm. Think about it. If they see you eating in an idol's temple, won't that trip them up in their consciences? Won't they be put into a moral dilemma? Won't they be tempted to violate their own consciences in order to do what you're doing? Do you really want their blood on your hands just because you have a knowledge and a freedom that they don't have? Jesus died for them; don't lead them into death just because you chose pride over love! When you sin against them in that way, you're sinning against the King Himself! That's why, if it were necessary, I would never eat meat again, if it meant I would keep from causing one of God's children to stumble.

9 In fact, I defer to you in more ways than that in order to keep you from stumbling. Think about my apostleship and the rights that come with it, and how I have given up those rights just so no one can question my motives. I am an apostle, am I not? Aren't I as free as anyone else? Haven't I seen our Lord Jesus Christ face to face? And aren't you my work in the Lord? If I'm not an apostle to anyone else, I am certainly *your* apostle. You're the very proof of my apostleship.

To those who would try to poke holes in me and my ministry, I would defend myself this way: Isn't it our right to receive food and drink from you? Yes, at a bare minimum. And isn't it our right to be able to marry if we want to? Peter's married, as are several other apostles. And is it only Barnabus and I who have to work a 9-to-5 in addition to our full-time status in ministry? Kings don't pay for their own wars. Farmers eat the fruit of their own harvest. Shepherds drink the milk from their own flock.

Don't just take my word for it. The Law of Moses backs me up on this. It says, "Don't muzzle the ox so it can't eat as it steps on the husk to break out the grain." Is it really the oxen God was concerned with? Or was He really saying that for our benefit? For us, of course. Whoever plows should plow with the hope of sharing in the reward, and whoever threshes should thresh with the hope of sharing in the reward. We planted spiritual seed among you, so it's not wrong of us to expect a harvest of material support. Even those who minister in the temple get to eat from what is brought to the temple; and those who serve at the altar eat from the offerings brought to the altar. Likewise the Lord has ordained that those who preach the message of the Gospel should be able to make a living from those who receive that message. Don't all of the others who minister to you have this right, too? If they expect you to support them, we should expect it all the more.

But the fact is, we've never exercised this right. We've never demanded financial remuneration from you, instead choosing to make ends meet on our own, with the Lord's help, of course. Why? So that the Gospel of Christ would not be impeded because of some perceived impure motive on our part. I haven't received gifts from you, nor have I written you that you should give them to me. I'd rather die than have somebody be able to claim that I'm taking pride in anything other than Jesus. Preaching the Gospel is not something I can boast in. It's a calling and a duty that has been imposed on me, and I'm in big trouble if I don't do it! If it were merely something I wanted to do, I would take money for it. But it's more like a chore that I'm entrusted to steward as a slave of Christ. I'm not requiring payment from you because I am receiving a different kind of pay: the knowledge that my presentation of the Gospel is pure and above reproach, a sign that I have not abused my authority.

I'm not a literal slave of any man, but I have offered myself figuratively as a slave to every man, so that I can win as many as possible to the King. To the ethnic Jews, I lived as an ethnic Jew, so that I could win ethnic Jews. To the Law-abiding Jews I lived as a Law-abiding Jew, so that I could win Law-abiding Jews. (Although, make no mistake, I am under no obligation to abide by the Mosaic Law.) To the Gentiles who didn't have that Law, I became one who had no Law, so that I could win those without the Law. And to the weak I became as one who is weak, so that I could win those who are weak. See, I do whatever I can to meet people where they are, to get on their level, to establish a common ground from which to develop relationship and begin to lead people further and further down the path of truth—this newly revealed truth about Jesus and what He has done for us. I'm so excited to be able to one day share in the joy of this Gospel with you and everyone else who has been impacted by my ministry.

Many people run when there's a race, but only one can win the prize. You need to run your race in such a way that you win it and get the prize. Professional athletes are disciplined, training hard and abiding by a strict regimen. Even so, they are going after a crown that is temporary and will eventually decay, but we are going after a crown that is permanent and indestructible. Yes, Church, I'm running a real race and fighting a real fight. I'm not just punching a speed bag or passing some time on the treadmill. Still, I do discipline my body as I discipline my spirit, so that, having preached to others, I will not find myself unproven and unqualified.

10 Furthermore, friends, I want to remind you of something. Our spiritual forefathers in the generation of Moses witnessed many signs and wonders that should have been more than enough to keep them on the right track. They also experienced pre-patterns of the Christian ordinances we observe today. They camped under the cloud and they passed through the Red Sea; this was their version of Baptism. And they ate the manna and drank from the rock; this was their version of Communion. Indeed, the Rock that they drank from was Christ Himself. The spiritual Source of their provision is the same spiritual Source of our provision.

Yet God wasn't happy with them, because they disobeyed Him. He annihilated most of them and left their bodies strewn all over the wilderness. Well, that should serve as an example to us. We'd better not go after the same things they went after. We need to guard ourselves against the kind of idolatry that they fell into. Remember the scriptural account said, "First they ate and drank, and then they got up and began to play." By "play" it's referring to sexual immorality. That's the quintessential sign of a depraved and rebellious heart. Well, what happened? God wiped out 23,000 of them in one day, that's what happened. That should be a pretty clear indication to us that we shouldn't do the same thing.

Neither should we be tempting the King with doubt and ingratitude, nor bringing a complaint against Him from a rebellious posture. When the Israelites tempted the Lord, He unleashed a bunch of poisonous snakes on them, and when they presumed to usurp His authority, He crushed them. Now, all of these accounts were written down to teach us a lesson, because we're at the end of the journey, and we need to stay on track now more than ever. So, if you think you're in good standing, be on guard in order to keep from falling. There's not one of you who has been tempted by anything that isn't common to others. But God is faithful, and He won't allow you to be tempted beyond your capacity to endure and overcome that temptation through Him. He always has an escape route planned.

So, friends, avoid idolatry like the plague. (Decide for yourselves if what I'm saying makes perfect sense; you're reasonable people.) Here we are, one people, the very Body of

Christ, united together. And we demonstrate that unity and allegiance to Him when we drink from the cup and eat the bread. To drink the cup is to commune with Him through the blood of the covenant, and to eat the bread is to commune with Him through His body. We are many people, but we all eat from one loaf, signifying that we are one body. Think about the people of Israel: they eat from the offerings brought to the altar; doesn't that make them one with each other as well?

Okay, so now you're going to go insert yourself into a pagan worship experience by partaking of their sacrifices? I don't think so. You can't take part in the Lord's Table and then turn right around and eat the demons' meal, too. Not that I'm saying the food or even the demons themselves amount to anything. It's just food, and it's just being offered to a fake god. Regardless, I don't want you associating with demons and the pagan activities offered to them. Are you trying to make the Lord jealous? Do you think you can flirt with disaster and come out on top? You may say, "There's nothing off-limits for me in the grace covenant," but that doesn't mean everything is beneficial or that it will build you up. Stop thinking about this in terms of your own liberty and start thinking about it from other folks' vantage points.

Now, just so you don't think I'm talking out of both sides of my mouth, let me be very clear. To simply eat this meat from the animals that have been sacrificed to idols is not a sin in and of itself, but to participate in or associate with the worship of these idols in any way is certainly sinful. Furthermore, to eat the meat in the presence of those who don't understand these finer points of Christian liberty, thereby causing them to stumble, also becomes sin. So, if you have some of this meat that has been sold in the market, and you're giving God thanks as the Source of that provision, feel free to eat it; it need not bother your conscience. After all, "everything on the earth has been put here by the Lord." And if an unbeliever invites you to dinner, feel free to go and eat whatever they serve, no questions asked. But if anyone says to you, "This food was offered to idols," then don't eat it, so there won't be any confusion as to where you stand on the issue of idol worship. In so doing, you may be inviting them to stop and think. Their consciences may well tell them what they're doing is wrong, but at least you won't be helping them make excuses for themselves by assuaging their consciences. Your own conscience should not be bothered by eating meat but by impeding someone else's path to the knowledge and grace of God. Therefore, whatever you do, whether you eat the meat or don't eat the meat, do it with God's glory in view. Don't be the one who keeps somebody from getting saved—whether a Jew or a Gentile—and don't be the one who causes a member of the Church to regress. I'm trying to be just this kind of person who makes it as easy as possible for people to see the truth of the Gospel, not looking out for myself, but desiring them to receive the benefit, which is the salvation of their souls. **11** So, imitate me in this, just as I am imitating Christ.

Friends, you have done well in maintaining the ordinances of corporate worship I laid out for you at the start. But now I need to give you further instruction. The principle I want you to understand and begin putting into practice is rooted in God's divine authority. And here is how that authority trickles down: God is the head of Christ, Christ is the head of man, and man is the head of woman. (We see this authority bear out specifically in the husband-wife relationship.) Man reflects God's glory, and in turn, woman reflects man's reflection of God's glory. The woman was made for the man, and came from man, and yet man comes through woman. There is no doubt the man and the woman were made distinct from each other, to complement each other.

Now, here is the principle to be derived from this lesson: we should do our best to act in accordance with God's established distinction between the man and the woman. This means, men, don't dress like women and wear your hair like women, and ladies, don't dress like men and wear your hair like men. These norms are defined by our cultures, and we in the Church don't want to give the world the impression, by rejecting these norms, that our men have a debased sense of manhood or that our women have a debased sense of womanhood.

Neither should you present yourself in such a way as to give a false impression that you're single if you're actually married. Married couples should carry themselves in a way that celebrates their marriage and the roles that come with that institution.

When men and women of God meet together to pray to the Lord and prophesy to one another, they should do so with clear consciences, knowing that they are reflecting God's design in the way they are presenting themselves. You tell me: if a man who is known to be part of the church is donning a feminine hairstyle, do you think that's the right kind of message to send to the world, and to the church? No, I didn't think so.

Now, let's have a talk about the way you're practicing the Lord's Supper. I don't know if you were expecting me to compliment you on this or what, but I definitely can't do that. Actually, I think your fellowship dinners may be doing more harm than good! You're divided into factions, and that should not be. (Of course, there has to be some level of division when some people are doing right and some people are doing wrong, so that those who are doing right may be noted and find approval.) When you meet together, you're not actually eating the *Lord's* Supper; you're each eating your own supper. Some are scarfing down meals fit for a king while others are going hungry. And some of you are getting drunk to boot! Don't you have your own homes to eat and drink in? How dare you desecrate the house of God by shaming those who have less, degrading the holy remembrance of our Lord's death? Like I said, I certainly can't approve of what you're doing.

Now, this is the proper protocol for observing the Lord's Supper. I received this directly from the Lord, and I have shared it with you before. The Lord Jesus, on the night He was betrayed, took some bread, and after giving thanks, He broke it and said, "Take this and eat it; this is My body, which is broken for you; do this to remember Me." In the same way, He took the cup, after supper, saying, "This cup is the new covenant in My blood. As often as you drink it, remember Me when you do." For every time you eat the bread and drink from the cup, you are testifying about the Lord's death, from now until He returns.

So, whoever eats the bread and drinks from the cup in a sacrilegious manner that is unworthy of Him, will be found guilty of tearing His body to pieces and draining it of its blood. Examine yourselves. If you can observe the meal with respect, with a clean conscience, then go ahead and eat and drink. But if you eat and drink disrespectfully, you need to know that you are bringing judgment onto yourself by not honoring the Lord's body. This is why many of you are weak and sick, and some have actually died. If we were judging ourselves appropriately, we would not have to be judged by God. But God's judgment is a form of discipline to us, so that we won't be condemned with the world in the end. So, once again, friends, when you eat this meal, wait until everyone arrives, and share the meal together in love and unity. If you're hungry and want to eat beforehand, do that at home before you gather, so that you won't incur judgment. (I'll wait until I get there to address the other particulars.)

12 Now about the gifts of the Spirit, I want you to know what's right and proper. You used to be pagans who were somehow or other enticed into worshipping idols that can't even speak. But the one true God does speak, and nobody who speaks by His Spirit would ever curse Jesus, and nobody can claim Jesus as Lord except by the Holy Spirit.

There's variety in the gifts, but only one Spirit who gives them. There's variety in the ministerial offices, but only one Lord Jesus who appoints them. And there's variety in the effects produced when we operate according to His will, but only one Father God who is behind the scenes continuously pulling the strings on all of it.

Now the Spirit gives each of us a gift that we are to exercise for the common good. These include: the word of wisdom, the word of knowledge, exceptional faith, special healing gifts, dynamic miracle-working power, prophecy, recognition of various spirits and spirit-influences, various languages, and the interpretation of languages. The one and only Holy Spirit gives all of these expressions of Himself to us in His infinite wisdom.

In the same way that a body has many parts, yet we still understand it's one body, so Christ is one Body with many Body parts. We were all buried in baptism into one Body by one Spirit. And we were all resuscitated to newness of life by the breath of that one Spirit. But even though we are one Body, as individuals we are Body parts. And we should never pridefully desire to be a Body part that God didn't design or ordain us to be. You never hear of a foot renouncing its membership in the body because it's not a hand, or an eye renouncing its membership because it's not an ear. If we were just one big eye, we wouldn't be able to hear anything. And if we were just one big ear, we wouldn't be able to smell anything. God has fashioned this Body just the way He wanted to, making us into the parts He wants us to be. If He made us all one thing, there wouldn't be a Body at all! But there are many parts, which together make up one Body. So, it's totally improper for an eye to claim that he doesn't need the hands, or for the ear to claim that she doesn't need the feet. On the contrary, every little part, even the ones that sometimes seem less important, are actually critical to the success of the whole Body. It's common to think of our unmentionables as less honorable than other parts of our body, and yet we take the greatest care to cover those parts. Meanwhile, we don't give a second thought to leaving the "honorable" parts of the body uncovered. Thus we show more honor to the less honorable and less honor to the more honorable. That's how it is with the Body of Christ. God designed it so that extra honor and care should be shown to those parts that seem to lack spiritual stature, so that the Body will be whole and healthy and vibrant. If one of us is suffering, we should all empathize. If one of us is honored, we should all rejoice.

Collectively, you make up the Body of Christ; individually, you are members of that Body. And God has put all these gifts in place in the Church: first apostles, second prophets, third teachers, then dynamic miracle-working power, extraordinary healing gifts, special ministry to those in need, gifts of administration, and various languages. Is everybody called to be an apostle? Is everybody called to be a prophet, or a teacher? Does everyone leave a trail of miracles behind? Does everyone have a special healing gift? Does everyone speak in other languages by the Spirit? Does everyone have the ability to interpret those languages? No. But we should all desire to receive the gifts of God that He deems are best for us. Even so, there is something that supersedes all the gifts, and without it the gifts are meaningless. I'm talking about *love*.

13 I could speak in every human language, or even angelic languages; if I don't have love, I'm mere noise, like a crashing cymbal who has separated himself from God's orchestra, unable to join in the pure music-making He desires. I could unravel mysteries with the world's strongest gift of prophecy, or reveal hidden secrets with an uncanny word of knowledge, or have a faith so exceptional that I could literally move mountains; if I don't have love, I amount to nothing. I could give everything I have to the poor, or sacrifice my body, taking pride in my suffering; if I don't have love, those kinds of sacrifices won't profit me anything.

See, love is not about showing off our gifts. It's a supernatural empowerment to put others first. Those who demonstrate God's love display patience and kindness. They are not jealous, boastful, arrogant, rude, selfish, or hot-tempered. They don't keep track of all the times they've been wronged. They don't take pleasure in others' misery; they are hooked on truth. They are quick to overlook others' mistakes, to see the best in others, to maintain a confident optimism, and to keep doing these things perpetually. Loving others in this way never backfires.

Prophecy won't be around forever. Neither will the language gifts and the word of knowledge. Why would we need these gifts once the time of perfection comes and we are able to see the

Lord face to face? Right now we have a partial knowledge, and our prophetic insight only gives us part of the whole picture. It's like looking in a mirror with a cloudy film on it. It's like growing from childhood to adulthood; when you're a kid you really only have a partial understanding of the way the world works, and when you grow up, things become clearer and you're not interested in the same sorts of activities. Right now I know parts of the story, but in that Day, when I get to look my Savior right in the eyes, I will know Him the same way He knows me! So you see, the love of God will last forever, unlike the gifts. In fact, faith and hope and love are all eternal; but the greatest of these is love.

14 Now, this is not an either-or proposition. Pursue love *and* desire the spiritual gifts. Particularly prophecy. See, when you speak in unknown languages, you're not communicating anything to anybody. You are speaking mysteries by the Spirit— mysteries, that is, to everyone except God, of course, who is the only One who understands what you're saying. On the other hand, when you prophesy, you're speaking to people, and the purpose of that communication should be to build up, encourage, and bring comfort. The one who speaks in an unknown language builds up himself, but the one who prophesies builds up the Church. I wish you all spoke in unknown languages, but I wish even more you all prophesied, because the one who prophesies is operating in a gift that is more beneficial to the Church than is the one who speaks in unknown languages (unless the message is interpreted, in which case the congregation would be built up either way).

Now friends, if I were to come to your gathering and just start speaking in an unknown language, what good would that do by itself, unless I followed it up with some clear disclosure of truth, or a word of knowledge, or a prophetic proclamation, or some teaching? Think about a musical instrument like a flute or a harp. If the musician didn't play that thing with purpose and distinctive clarity, you wouldn't be able to pick out the melody. And if the bugler doesn't blast the right call, the soldiers won't know they're supposed to prepare for battle. That's the way it is with unknown languages. Unless you speak in a way that everyone can understand, nobody will get the message. You're just speaking it into the air. There are lots of languages in the world, and each one is essential to the ones who speak it, but if I don't know the language of the one talking, we're foreigners to each other.

Nevertheless, I know you're very excited about the gifts, and the language gift in particular. So, by all means, ask the Lord for it, and exercise it if you have it, but just make sure you are asking for and operating in the gifts in order to build up the church. So, for example, the one who speaks in an unknown language should pray for the ability to interpret so that gift may benefit the others. If I pray in an unknown language, it's my spirit that's praying, and my mind doesn't know what I'm praying. Well, it makes sense, then, that we should pray with our spirits *and also* pray in a language we can understand. Likewise, we can sing from our spirits *and also* sing intelligibly. If you proclaim your praises in the spirit, how can an uninitiated visitor, having no idea what you're saying, come into agreement with your declaration of thanksgiving? You may very well be a praise machine, but you're not doing a good job at building up others. I praise God, too, because I speak in unknown languages more than all of you. But in a congregational setting, I would rather speak five words we all understand, so that you may be taught something, rather than 10,000 words none of us can understand.

Church, be as innocent as babies when it comes to wrongdoing, but when it comes to spiritual matters like this, you need to have the mature understanding of full-grown adults. This is what God said in His Word: "I will speak to these people through foreigners who will communicate in other languages, and yet they will still not hear what I have to say." See, these unintelligible languages are a sign of judgment against those who refuse to believe. But prophecy is a sign of reconciliation directed at those who will heed it. When you're gathered together, if everyone starts speaking in unknown languages, the unbelieving visitors will simply say you're cuckoo. But if an unbeliever hears you prophesy, and his deepest darkest secrets are revealed, he will surely be convicted, and he may very well fall down on his face in repentance and worship God. Then the report will go out that God is in your midst.

Okay, let's nail down a bit more about proper order in the congregational gatherings. First, when the church gathers, no doubt each one who comes will bring a song, or a teaching, or a revelation from God, or a word in an unknown language, or the interpretation of a word. All of these serve as beautiful, multi-faceted evidence that God is at work there; so be sure that it is all done for the express purpose of building up the church. If the gift of unknown languages is in operation, let two or three, at most, speak in turn, and be sure to wait on the interpretation to come. If no interpretation is given, let the one who spoke discontinue speaking before the congregation and instead exercise that gift between himself and God. Similarly, let two or three prophets speak, leaving space for the others to evaluate what is said. If, while one is prophesying, another receives revelation, let the baton be passed. No one should have a monopoly on the Word of the Lord. Everybody may prophesy, one by one, so that everybody can gain something and be encouraged by it. And there is no reason why anyone should feel so emboldened to prophesy that they usurp these protocols; the spirit of prophecy is completely controlled by the one prophesying. God made it this way because He is all about peace and order, not distress and confusion. Now, this is the way it is for all of the churches everywhere.

Your women have a desire to learn; that's wonderful! Just make sure that they're not asking their questions out loud right in the middle of church. That would be disruptive and out of order. Instead, let them ask their husbands later on, when such a conversation is more appropriate. This would be the proper way to demonstrate a submissive spirit.

Now, that's all I have to say on the subject of order in the congregational gathering. I trust you will take seriously the protocols I've laid out and diligently put them into practice. I hope you're not so arrogant that you think the Gospel originated in Corinth, or that you're the only ones God has reached with it. No, it's much more widespread than the little world you know there. So, I guess if there's anyone there who thinks himself a prophet, he'll be able to perceive that what I've said here is all legit. And the ones who are clueless will be clueless. Whatever. Bottom line: be eager to prophesy *and also* continue to allow for the gift of unknown languages to operate; and be sure that it's all done appropriately and orderly.

15 Finally, let me address the question of the resurrection of the dead, because some are saying there won't be a resurrection, and I need to correct that thinking. Let's start with the Gospel itself, which is totally dependent on *Jesus'* resurrection. Here is that Gospel—the message I received from the Lord, the same message I preached to you in the beginning, the message you received and by which you are saved and in which your position is fixed (assuming your faith is genuine):

Jesus, the Messiah, died to solve the problem of sin, fulfilling all the biblical prophecies related to that act. He was buried, and He rose again on the third day. That, too, was predicted in the Scriptures. After His resurrection, people saw Him with their own eyes. Peter saw Him. The twelve disciples saw Him. After that He was seen by 500 people simultaneously; and most of those people are still alive today, so the accuracy of the eyewitness testimony can still be verified! After that He was seen by James, and then all the other apostles. And lastly, He appeared to me, the one born in a different time. (I am the most insignificant of the apostles, utterly unworthy of that title. The fact that I hunted down and murdered Christians should have disqualified me from ministry, but God's grace completely changed my heart and mind and empowered me to serve Him how He sees fit. I've worked harder than anyone else He has called. Not that I would really give myself the credit, it's God's grace that is working in me to accomplish His desires.) So whether I preached to you, or one of the other apostles did, the point is you heard the Gospel preached and you believed.

Now, if Jesus rose again after He died, why are some of you claiming that we won't rise again after we die? I'm telling you, the resurrection of Christ and the resurrection of His followers are inextricably linked. If we're not going to be raised, then Christ wasn't raised, and if He's not risen, then everything we're doing is in vain. We would have to be considered false witnesses about God in that case, because our testimony is the resurrection of Christ, and if we are not raised back to life, then He was never raised back to life. Not only would we be believing a lie, if Jesus were not alive, we would still be dead in our sins, our faith would have no basis in reality, and those who have died in Christ would be suffering the eternal death. If the promise of Christ is for this life only, we're a sad, sorry bunch.

But, of course, Jesus *did* rise again, He *is* alive. And His resurrection is the initial evidence of the great resurrection to come. Since death came through a man, it makes sense that the resurrection of the dead would also come through a man. We all have descended from Adam, and every one of us inherited from him the malignant spiritual genetic defect called *sin*. But the sinless Jesus beat death, and those who trust in Him will be made alive. This is the order, though: first, Christ, the beginning of the harvest; afterward, everyone who belongs to Him will rise again when He returns. That's when the end will come, when He renders inactive all natural and spiritual powers and authorities, and hands the kingdom over to Father God. See, He will exercise His kingly power until all of the imposters have been subjugated. And the last of these enemies to be conquered will be death. Now, the Bible says, "God has put all things under His feet," though obviously God Himself is excluded from the *all* in "all things," since He's not going to put Himself under His own feet. No, when everything comes under the total control of King Jesus in the last Day, then He will subject Himself to the Father, who put everything under the Son's control in the first place. In this God will complete His great master plan, and we will all understand that He is and always has been the sum total of ultimate reality.

Look, if there's no resurrection, what will become of those who are baptized for the dead? What would be the point of that practice? And if there's no resurrection, why do we keep subjecting ourselves to the threat of execution for our faith? I'm coming up against that threat of death daily; it's as real to me as the assurance I have in the work Christ Jesus is doing in you. And if the fight I put up against the wild beasts who came against me in Ephesus were born out of my own human desires and mindset, there would have been no point to it either. There's no point to any of it without the resurrection. Isaiah commented on the futility: "We might as well throw a party, 'cause tomorrow we're all dead." People of God, don't think like this! Even the secular philosophers know that "Keeping company with evil will begin to wear away at any good in you." Wake up and begin to do what you know is right. Stop sinning! I'm telling you, some of you don't even know God. Shame on you.

I can hear you now: "How exactly are we going to be resurrected, and what kind of bodies will we have?" What a foolish question. When you grow crops, you don't plant a whole ear of corn or a big juicy tomato in the ground. You put a single seed, a single kernel, and that seed, that kernel, has to be dead before it can come to life in the desired form. And God gives each seed its own body, as He pleases.

Different creatures have different body types: man has one type, land animals another, fish another, and birds yet another. There's also a notable difference between the kinds of bodies that are native to earth and those that are in the heavens. They each have different degrees of splendor. And the sun and the moon and each individual star all have differing degrees of brightness. Now, that's the way it is with resurrected bodies. The physical body is planted in the ground in death, and it's raised into eternal life as a spiritual body. Where there is a physical body, there is a spiritual body. It's planted in darkness and raised in brilliance; it's planted in weakness and raised in strength.

The Scriptures tell us, "God gave the first man, Adam, a physical form, and then made him into a living being." But the last Adam—that is, Christ—is a life-giving Spirit. See, the spiritual doesn't come first; the natural comes first, then the spiritual. The first man came from earth, being made from dust; the last Man came from heaven and exists eternally. Everyone has a body like Adam's, but those who are born into Christ's Family will be given a heavenly body like His. In the same way we look like Adam in this life, we'll look like Jesus in the next life.

Church, what I'm telling you is, flesh-and-blood bodies can't inherit God's kingdom, nor can what is prone to decomposition inherit what will never decay. Look, there's mystery to all this, no doubt. But you can believe this: we won't all die, but we *will* all undergo this transformation, in an instant, in the blink of an eye, at the last trumpet. When that trumpet blasts, the dead will be raised, and both the living and the dead will be transformed, receiving glorified bodies that will never again decompose. Our dying bodies have to be transformed into indestructible ones; our mortality has to give way to immortality. Once that happens, these words of the prophets will be fulfilled: "Victory gulps down death" leading us to say, "Hey, death, what happened there? Here I am walking away without a scratch. Hey, grave, how 'bout that? Looks like you couldn't quite hang on for the win ... loser." See, the way death strikes is through sin, and what gives sin its power is the Law, which almost begs to be broken. But, praise God! He gives us freedom from the Law and victory over sin through our Lord Jesus Christ. So, my dear brothers and sisters, be resolute and unwavering, vigorously working for the Lord, knowing that your efforts are not in vain.

16 Now about the fund we're collecting for the saints in need, I'm telling you the same thing I told the Galatians: each of you should set aside what you can at the first of each week; that way we won't have to scrounge up a collection when I come; it'll already be ready to go. Then when I arrive, I'll send letters off with the ones you decide on to deliver the gift, and we'll send them to Jerusalem. If we get the feeling that I should go with them, I can do that, too.

I'll be visiting you when I pass through Macedonia. That's the plan anyway. I might be able to stay awhile with you, maybe even all winter. Then, wherever I end up going after that, you can give me a proper sendoff. I don't really want this to be a quick visit. I'd like to be able to spend some good quality time there if the Lord allows. For now, I'll be hanging out in Ephesus, at least until Pentecost. God has opened a substantial door here for me that's really making an impact, although I'm also getting a lot of opposition.

When Timothy gets there, don't give him any cause for concern, because he's doing the Lord's work just as I am. Don't let anybody show disrespect to him. When it comes time for him to return, send him off with your blessing, because I'm expecting to see him again, as well as the other believers.

I tried to talk Apollos into making a trip to see you, along with the others, but he was pretty insistent on not coming right now. He *will* come though, at a more opportune time.

Here's the final word: pay attention; stay persistent in the faith; be brave; keep getting stronger and stronger; do everything from a posture of love.

I'm so glad that Stephanus and Fortunatus and Achaicus were able to come see me. If I can't see you all, at least I have had them here to encourage me. And they have been an encouragement to you, too. So be sure you show them the honor they deserve. Guys, I'm serious about this: you really need to submit to Stephanus, and others like him, who work for the Lord with us. You know Stephanus. He and his household were the first believers in all of southern Greece, and they have devoted their lives to serving God's holy people. Honor him for his service.

The churches in Turkey send their greetings. Aquila and Priscilla and everyone in their house church send a heartfelt "God bless you." All of our brothers and sisters everywhere say "Hello." Greet each other in the love of Christ.

This is me, Paul, signing off with my own hand. Let anyone who does not love the Lord Jesus Christ be cursed. *Maranatha!* Lord, come! May the grace of the Lord Jesus Christ envelop you. Love to all, in Christ Jesus. Amen.

Discussion Questions

WEEK 13: 1 Corinthians 1-6

- This letter opens with a rebuke regarding cliques and the divisiveness caused by following after certain leaders. Can you think of a similar problem in today's Christianity?

- We have read many passages that indicate that people who call themselves Christians and yet continue to engage in carnal behavior will not make it to heaven. At the beginning of this letter, however, Paul indicates that his audience is "holy" and "in Christ" (1:2) and yet still carnal (3:3). Is there such a thing as a carnal Christian? Wrestle with this a bit.

- Paul instructs the Corinthian church to excommunicate one of its members who was unrepentantly engaging in bad behavior (Chapter 5). Discuss the nuance between Jesus' statement that we "judge not" (Matt 7:1) and the Church's authority and even duty to judge its members.

- "Unrighteous people will not inherit God's kingdom," according to 1 Cor 6. The list of sins given after this statement are accurately rendered in the paraphrase. Consider the contrast between Christian living and worldly living.

WEEK 14: 1 Corinthians 7-11

- Chapters 8-10 give Paul's extensive response to the question of "meat offered to idols." What modern-day scenarios could you come up with that might be analogous to the point Paul is making here?

- In Chapter 10 we get a warning: If God destroyed the Israelites because of their disobedience, won't He do the same to us? Does this stir anything up in you? Explain.

- Read 1 Cor 11:2-16 in a good translation. Discuss some possible reasons for the fairly wide departure from the original text presented in the paraphrase.
- When Paul says "examine yourself" in 1 Cor 11:28, do you think he had in mind a little contemplative prayer where we casually ask forgiveness for anything we might have done wrong that week? What is the broader problem he's concerned with here?

WEEK 15: 1 Corinthians 12-16

- Chapters 12-14 comprise the longest discussion of spiritual gifts in all of Paul's writings. Do you know what your spiritual gift(s) are? Are you using them in an orderly way? Are you using them to "build up" the church?
- In the middle of this discussion of spiritual gifts, Paul explains that love is the driving force behind the operation of all gifts. Have you ever found yourself pursuing your own gifts more than love? Have you ever caught yourself admiring someone's gift who didn't have the fruit to go along with it? Why is this dangerous?
- Why does Paul consider the gift of prophecy to be greater than the gift of unknown languages (also known as *tongues*)?
- Paul considered the resurrection of Jesus to be central to the Gospel and the evidence of our own resurrection (Chapter 15). Explain why the resurrection of the dead at the time of Jesus' return is so important.

PAUL'S SECOND LETTER TO THE
CORINTHIANS

1 To all of God's children in Corinth and the surrounding regions,

This is Paul, a man chosen by God to be an apostle of King Jesus, and Timothy, your brother in the Spirit, wishing you grace and peace from God our Father and the Lord Jesus Christ.

I praise God, the Father of our Lord Jesus Christ, this Father who is exceedingly merciful and comforting. He consoles us when we feel the overwhelming pressure of tribulation, so that we, in turn, may console others in their troubles with the same comfort He shows us. The more we suffer the way Christ did, the more He will comfort us in our time of need. When we endure the affliction imposed by evil men, like olives being crushed to make oil, it really becomes a source of comfort and salvation to you. The same is true when we are comforted through those tough times. Our example of hardship as well as comfort-in-hardship will serve you well as you endure the same suffering we have. We're confident in your ability to endure, because we know that suffering will not come without consolation.

Friends, we want to bring you up to speed on the trouble we ran into in Turkey. It got so bad that we felt sure we were going to die. The load was really more than we could bear. It forced us into a new level of trust in the God who raises the dead. He was truly our only hope. He delivered us from death, and He will deliver us again. And your prayers are helping to effect our deliverance. When it's all said and done, everyone will thank God for the work He did on our behalf through all of the Church's prayers.

We don't mind telling people that we have never violated our consciences as we have consistently lived simple, godly lives. We don't rely on our own wisdom, but only on God's grace. And this is especially true in the way we have interacted with you. We haven't tried to hide anything from you in what we've written. I know you've been able to grasp at least some of what we've taught you, and I trust you will come to realize how proud we are going to be of each other—you of us and we of you—when the Lord returns.

That's why I wanted to come to Corinth. Actually, I wanted to come twice, once on the way to Macedonia, and once on the way back. Then you would have had double the benefit, and you could have happily sent me back to Judea. Now, I didn't plan all that on a whim. I'm not in the habit of saying I'm going to do one thing and then doing another. In the same way God doesn't waffle between "yes" and "no," we endeavor not to waffle between "yes" and "no." (The Son of God whom we preached to you—we: Timothy, Silas, and I—there's not a "yes" and a "no" in Him, but only a big fat "yes." He is the "Yes!" that fulfills all of God's promises; all we have to do is yield fully to Him with our sincere response of "Amen!" God is glorified by this. God empowers us all to stand firm in Christ, anointing us, affixing His seal of ownership in the wax of our hearts, and giving us the Holy Spirit as a deposit on all that is to come.)

So, believe me when I say that the only reason I didn't return to Corinth was that I didn't want to have to bring even more rebuke. That's the truth, with God as my witness. It's not our job to strong-arm you in spiritual matters, although we're not going to sugar coat the painful truth either. You have to make your own choices, and you have to live out your own faith in integrity. We're just here to help you along as much as we can. **2** So, I decided I would not come give you another tongue-lashing. If I keep hurting you, even if it's the kind of pain that's necessary to bring positive change, I won't have anybody to encourage me. So, I sent you that scathing letter instead, hoping that it would do the trick, and when I actually do get to come, we can have a pleasant visit instead of a painful one. Writing that letter was gut-wrenching and brought me to tears. I didn't write it to make you feel bad, but because I love you enough to candidly present my assessment of the egregious practices you were hanging on to.

Now, the guy who caused all the trouble there definitely had more of a negative impact on you than he had on me. I'm not just saying that. But he felt the sting of correction, which had majority support, and that's all the situation required. Now's the time to forgive and come around this man with the love of God that forges reconciliation. Otherwise he'll have to suffer undue heartbreak. I'm telling you, reaffirm him in love. I wrote to you as a sort of test, to see if you would be obedient in bringing correction. Now the test is whether you can also be obedient in bringing reconciliation. I forgive anyone you forgive. And, in particular, I have forgiven this man, with Christ looking on, so that Satan can't use this as an opportunity to get his claws into us. We know his methods.

I wish you could understand the weight I feel as your apostle. For example, God had opened the door for me to minister in Troas, so I went. But I was almost too concerned over you to be effective there. See, Titus was supposed to meet me to report on your response to my letter. But he didn't show. So I was left in the dark, and continued to agonize over you until I eventually moved on to Macedonia. Do you see what I mean? Being responsible for all of these churches is a big job that I wouldn't wish on anyone.

On the other hand, I wouldn't trade it for the world! I'm so grateful to have this honor, even though it comes with tremendous heartache. God has conquered me and made me His slave, and He drags me around behind His victory parade, showing me off to the whole world. My old carnal self hates it, because it means a daily death sentence. But for the new me—

the real me—it's a badge of honor. One thing's for sure: God is getting all the glory out of my life, because I'm sure not getting any!

We are the sweet aroma that wafts up to God's nostrils from Christ's sacrifice—the only truly efficacious brazen-altar offering ever to be burned up. And people everywhere are picking up our scent. To those who are being saved, we are the fresh fragrance of life; but to those who are headed toward damnation, we are the foul stench of death. Only someone like me, who has been conscripted by the Master into forced labor, can be equal to such a task. That's why I preach the Word of God with integrity and sincerity, knowing that the King sees everything I'm doing. I won't lower myself to use the Gospel as a mere tool for making money.

3 Do we really have to rehash all our credentials? Are you going to make us send in reference letters as if we're complete unknowns? You *are* our reference letter. You're the very work that we get to list on our résumé. You're not written on paper. You're written in our hearts. When people see you, they know they're reading our writing. Actually, not even ours—you're really a letter written by the King Himself; we're just taking dictation for Him. He didn't write the story of your salvation with ink but by the Spirit of the living God; He didn't carve it into stone tablets but onto human hearts. We're confident that God gives us everything we need to be competent and sufficient to carry out the ministry He's given us. It's not a self-confidence, mind you, but a confidence in Him.

We are ministers of the *New* Covenant. We don't follow the letter of the Law, but rather the Spirit behind it. That Spirit breathes life into those who follow Him, but those who follow the letter of the Law are headed toward death—not that it's the Law's fault they're dying; it's the sin that rears its ugly head when the Law confronts them that's to blame. Moses' ministry, based on the letter of the Law, which was literally etched in stone, led to death. And yet the Israelites couldn't even look Moses straight in the face because of the brightness of the glory that radiated from it. Do you really think such a ministry could be more glorious than the ministry of the Spirit who brings life? No way. That glory faded away, but the glory of the Spirit will never fade away. To whatever degree the old system was glorious, the new system is infinitely more glorious. There's no comparison between the old and the new. The eternal always outweighs the temporal.

It's because we have a hope anchored in this eternal glory that we speak with such boldness. Moses hid his glory because the Israelites couldn't stand the brightness, even though it was fading away. Still to this day they are blinded to the true glory of God, because the veil still covers their hearts. When the writings of Moses are read, when the Law and the Prophets are read, the veil is still draped over their hearts, because only through Christ does that veil get removed. But when one turns to the Lord, the veil is taken away. This Lord who takes away the veil is the Spirit, so the very presence of the Lord's Spirit brings this tremendous freedom. Now *we* have had *our* faces unveiled, and we are mirroring the glory of the Lord, seeing it and reflecting it and becoming more and more like it. His glory in us is not waning. It's increasing as His Spirit continues to make us look more like Him.

4 Since God in His mercy has given us this new system marked by freedom in Him, we keep moving forward without letting ourselves get discouraged. We don't do shameful things in secret places. We're not schemers. We handle the Word of God with integrity. We present the plain truth and let it speak for itself. You know deep down that's all the character witness we need, and God knows it, too.

Of course, for those headed toward death, who do not believe, the Gospel we preach still has a veil over it. They're not able to see it because the devil is blocking out the light of the Gospel of the glory of Christ, who is the Image of God. We don't preach the greatness of Paul and Timothy. We preach the Lordship of King Jesus. And we make it clear that we are merely serving you on His behalf. The God who said, "Let there be light," has also turned on the light in our hearts by showing us the glory of God in the face of Jesus Christ.

But that treasure, that light, that glory, has been poured into the lowliest of vessels. All the torture and adversity we've endured has made our bodies weak and tired. They're not the crystal stemware you might expect God would think worthy of holding His glory. They're more like disposable paper cups. But that's just the point. It's because our lives are so unappealing that God's glory has been so evident through us. There's no mistaking it's all Him and no us in this operation!

And He is sustaining us despite the major difficulties we're facing. We're feeling the pressure from all sides, but it's not crushing us. Supplies are scarce, but we're not completely destitute. We're mistreated, but God hasn't abandoned us. We've taken a few beat downs, but they haven't killed us yet. Our suffering and inevitable death make us associates of the Lord Jesus, and His life-giving power is on display in us through that association. I know there are some who still think their prosperous lifestyle proves their brand of Christianity is better than ours, but they're flat wrong. It's because of the death we're enduring that you even have life.

We resonate with the psalmist who said, "I believed, therefore I spoke." Since we have the same spirit of faith he had, we aren't afraid to speak what we believe. Death doesn't bother us because we believe that the One who raised Jesus from the dead will raise us from the dead, too. And when He does, He'll bring you into fellowship with us. Yes, everything going on with us is being done for your sake, so that grace may spread, gratitude may ensue, and God may ultimately receive all the glory.

So we're not giving up. Even though we're literally dying on the outside, we're thriving more and more each day on the inside. The suffering we're having to endure is so short-lived and inconsequential compared to the awesome, thick, heavy glory that we will get to enjoy for eternity. That's why we choose to ignore all the negatives in the natural realm and focus on all the positives in the spiritual realm, because what we can see is only temporary, but the unseen realm of the spirit is eternal.

5 And if our bodies are slaughtered, who cares? They're merely tents compared to the sturdy, permanent housing we'll receive afterward. We'll be enjoying those glorified bodies in heaven for all eternity. It's pretty miserable to be living in these bodies right now, but we're looking forward to putting on our glorified bodies like a fresh suit of clothes, because we won't be the ones who are left naked after death. We can't help but groan a bit from the strain we're under. But we're not looking just to get rid of our ragged clothes, we're looking to put on the new ones. We're not looking to die for the sake of dying, we just know that death will give way to the better life. God has prepared us for all of this, and He's given us His Spirit as a guarantee that the rest is all coming.

So we maintain a confidence, knowing that as long as we stay in these bodies we are being kept from seeing the Lord. But because our life is a life of faith, and we don't have tunnel vision on the tangible world around us, we're more than just confident, we're actually excited at the prospect of trading these bodies in on the new ones so that we can be with the Lord.

And that's why we are always aspiring to please God in everything we do. We know that everyone is going to have to appear before the King on the Day when He sits in judgment. Each of us will be evaluated based on what we have done in this life, whether good or bad. Since we know full well the terror that lies in wait for those who are found guilty, we preach the singular way of escape—the Lordship of Jesus Christ—in hopes of persuading many to repent. But God knows that we are among the ones who will be rewarded for our faithfulness. And we trust that you know it, too.

We're not saying all this to make ourselves look good. We're saying it so that you understand that you have a legitimate reason to be proud of us, and so you will know how to rebut those who claim that the measure of God's favor lies in external success rather than the condition of the heart. For those who think we're out to lunch, we'll just let God be the Judge; for those who understand that what we're saying is the truth, you'll be able to benefit from it. It's Christ's love that moves on us to do what we're doing and say what we're saying. We are convinced that Jesus' death precipitates a death-by-association of the old carnal self, for everyone who belongs to Him. So let's stop living according to our own petty desires. He died for us all so that we could live *for Him*—and don't forget, He came back to life, too!

We used to be like these other ministers who evaluate everyone purely from a natural viewpoint. In fact, we evaluated Jesus that way once upon a time! But not anymore. We know Him intimately now. And in that knowing, He gives us the spiritual acumen to be able to evaluate people from the Holy Spirit's viewpoint.

Yes, those who are in Christ are totally new creations. All the old ways have become things of the past. Everything in the believer's life is of God, truly new and improved. God has reconciled us to Himself through Jesus Christ. In other words, God was actually made incarnate in the Person of Christ in order to perform the act of reconciliation and secure our forgiveness from sin. And He's given *us* the task of preaching that message of reconciliation. So, here we are, the King's ambassadors, writing to you as though God Himself were pleading with you: on Christ's behalf we implore you to be reconciled to God! Don't you see how important it is? Don't you see how astounding the steps were that He took to make our salvation possible? He actually made the sinless Jesus *to be sin* in our place, so that through Him we could become the righteousness of God. **6** That's why we're working with Him to plead with you not to spit in the face of God's grace. He said, "I heard you at the right time; I helped you on the day of salvation." Well, now is the right time, and today is the day of salvation!

We don't do anything that would cause anyone to be able to point the finger and say we're not representing God well. On the contrary, everything we do proves we are the kind of servants God is pleased with. We have endured severe adversity, calamity and anguish, near-fatal wounds, stints in prison, tumultuous living conditions, hard labor, sleepless nights, and extended periods with no food.

Yet we continue to prove ourselves by staying pure, growing in the knowledge of God, and demonstrating patience and kindness and sincere love in the Holy Spirit. Whether by speaking the truth or by demonstrating God's power or by defending ourselves and attacking the enemy with righteousness, we are serving Him always. We keep pressing forward whether we're honored or dishonored, praised or reviled, VIP's or complete unknowns, thought to be genuine or thought to be charlatans. We're dying, but we're still living. We're getting scourged, but we haven't been executed yet. We're grieved, yet we're joyful. We're poor, yet we're making lots of people rich in God. We have nothing, and yet we have it all.

Oh, Corinthians! We've told you everything! We're not keeping any secrets! We love you and we're for you! Why don't you love us in return? I'm speaking to you right now as if you were my own children: receive us, as people and as ministers, without reservation. You owe us that much.

Don't allow yourself to be tied to these faithless people. What kind of relationship does righteousness have with lawlessness? When do light and darkness ever get together for a visit? What are all the points that The Anointed One and The Treacherous One agree on? What portion of the things of God is shared by believers and unbelievers? And since when does the Temple of God give assent to idols? Don't you know you *are* God's Temple?! He said, "I will live in them and walk among them. I will be their God, and they will be My people." Therefore, "Get away from these people," says the Lord, "and stay separate from them. If you will keep from touching what is unclean, I will give you favor. I will be your Father, and you will be my sons and daughters, says the Lord Almighty." **7** Since we have these promises, friends, let's get rid of all the filth that pollutes our bodies and spirits so that we can be holy through and through.

Open up a place in your hearts for us to settle in and be cherished. We haven't done anybody wrong. We haven't led anyone astray. We haven't taken advantage of anyone. Look, I'm not trying to make you feel guilty. I've told you before that you are so deeply established in our hearts that we would gladly walk all the way to the executioner with you, or conversely, if we were able, we would gladly do life with you. I'm telling you like it is: I'm very proud of you, I'm very encouraged by your progress and faithfulness. In spite of our affliction, you Corinthians provide me a never-ending supply of joy.

When we arrived in Macedonia, we found no relief from the persecution that came at us from all different directions. Externally we faced contentious people; internally we faced our own fears. But the God who cheers us up when we're down sent Titus, just in the nick of time. And cheer us up he did, not just by the fact that we got to reunite with our dear friend, but also because of the good news he brought us about you. When he told me about how much you wished you could see me, how sorry you were about what was happening to me, and your concern for my wellbeing, it was so encouraging to me. Knowing that my letter produced the kind of godly conviction that leads to repentance made it worth the pain of sending it. I hated to have to send it, because I knew it would be painful to you, and I don't like causing people pain. But some pain is necessary, and in this case, you needed to feel that godly sorrow in order to move forward to the place God wanted you to be. So, there are no regrets wherever godly sorrow produces repentance leading to salvation. (By contrast, the sorrow of the world's system is totally different. The way of the world heaps condemnation on you, and it offers no escape, only death.) You need look no further than your own situation to see the truth in what I'm saying. You were sorry, in a good way, for the things you did that were wrong, and look at all the positives that came from it: dedication to me, indignation at the offense and a dedication to making things right, a godly fear and a zeal and a desire to do right. Obviously you've made up for everything that went wrong. And that's why I wrote the letter. It wasn't as much to call out the one who did wrong or the one who got wronged as it was to show you how devoted to us you really are. And you did prove it to yourselves, and to God.

So, we're happy you're happy. And we're even happier that Titus is happy. He was really refreshed in his spirit by his visit with you. I had bragged to him about you before, and now, I'm glad I don't have to retract all the good things I said about you. I always tell the truth, and apparently my account of the Corinthians was true, too! And Titus has a soft spot in his heart for you now, as he can reflect back on the godly angst you demonstrated, being unsure whether you were equal to the task, but willing to give it your best shot and be obedient. Hearing that thrills me, because I finally have a complete confidence in you.

8 Now, church, I'm calling on you to give financially to support our brothers and sisters in Judea who are impoverished. I want to remind you of the example the Macedonian churches have set for you in this. God graced them, in the middle of their miserable trial, to give beyond their ability—they themselves being quite poor—of their own free will, from a joyful heart. They insisted on contributing to the Lord's people who were in even worse shape, understanding what a great privilege it was. Their giving was more than we could have expected. They gave their whole selves to God as the One who had first place in their hearts, and they have completely submitted themselves to us, too. This was God's will.

So, we prompted Titus, who was the driving force in getting your collection started in the first place, to come encourage you to finish this project of grace you started. You've been doing a great job in everything—in your faithfulness, in the way you speak, in gaining knowledge, in being diligent, and in the way you love us. So, we're asking you to do a great job in giving, too.

This is not a commandment from the King I'm relaying to

you; it's my own imperative. I want you to follow the lead of the Macedonians, demonstrating sincere love and diligence as they have. The Lord Jesus Christ is another obvious example to you in this. He demonstrated His grace to you by laying down His infinite riches to become poor, so that you could become rich through His poverty. So, pick up where you left off last year with your alms collection, not just because I'm saying so, but because you truly want to. And don't worry about how much you're giving. If the desire to give is there, the gift is measured in terms of what you have, not what you don't have. And don't think we're saying you should give so much that you end up destitute while the people you're giving to end up having more. No, this is about all God's children working to meet each others' needs. Right now, you have it and they don't. A time may come when they have it and you don't. Then the shoe will be on the other foot. The account of the Israelites in the wilderness is instructive here: "The ones who gathered more than necessary had no leftovers, and the ones who didn't gather much still had enough."

Praise God! He put the same genuine devotion I have for you into Titus' heart. Titus was more than happy when we asked him to return to you to steward the collection process, and with great zeal, he went willingly. We sent another brother with him whose commitment to the Gospel has earned him a stellar reputation in all the churches. He was actually the one the churches picked to go with us to deliver the joint collection from all the churches (after your contribution has been added). We'll be administering this gift in the Lord's honor. We're eager to do so. And we certainly don't want to give anyone any reason to criticize our handling of this large gift. We've thought long and hard about how to do this the right way. That's why we're sending several vetted men of God to take responsibility. The third brother has proved himself zealous for the Lord, and he demonstrated great confidence in *you*, that you would come through for us in this. If anyone questions these three, know this: Titus is my partner in ministry and works closely with me on a regular basis, in particular on your account. And the other two brothers are hand-picked representatives of the other churches, who manifest the very glory of Christ. So, treat them right, demonstrate God's love toward them, and show everyone in the worldwide Church that everything we've said about you is true.

9 Now, I don't really need to say anything about this gift we're putting together for the saints. I know that you're willing to give. I'm always telling the Macedonians, "Southern Greece was ready a year ago." And because of your zeal, most of your neighbors to the north are on board, too. But I sent these brothers to make sure you're ready, so that all the bragging we're doing on you doesn't turn out to be unfounded. On the chance that some Macedonians come with me and find you unprepared, you and I both would be embarrassed, wouldn't we? So, I thought it prudent to send these brothers in advance to ensure that your collection is regularly accumulating. You promised the gift previously, and we want you to be ready, so it can be given generously and cheerfully, not resentfully.

And I'll say this: whoever sows very little will reap very little, and whoever sows a lot will reap a lot. So, each one of you needs to decide in your heart what to give. It needs to be an amount that you can give freely and happily, not reluctantly, because God loves a happy giver. There's no cap on His grace toward someone who gives. Givers get resupplied; their own needs are met, and they have more leftover to keep giving. As the psalmist wrote: "He has spread his riches out all over. He has given to the poor. His righteousness persists forever."

So, may the God who gives us seed to plant and bread to eat, give you seed and turn it into a bountiful harvest, the fruits produced from righteous acts. And God will continue to give back to you on every front, so that you may continue to give generously every time it's called for. And God will be thanked because of you. So, not only will the needs of God's people be met, but God will be praised in the process. Because of your faithfulness in this task and the testimony of the Gospel that it proves, God will be glorified. And the ones you're helping will have a soft spot in their hearts for you when they pray because of the prominence of God's grace in you. *Thank you, Lord, for your indescribable gift!*

10 This is specifically Paul talking now. I'm begging you, in the humility and gentleness of Christ, to make the changes necessary so that I won't have to come down strong on you the next time I see you. I know you think I just talk a big game in my letters and never follow through by putting the hammer down when I'm with you in person. But right now I'm expecting to have to be stern when I come, because I will not tolerate people saying that we maintain worldly lifestyles. We may live in flesh-and-bone bodies, but we do not live in a way that satisfies the appetites of our flesh. And we don't fight using the world's tactics either. We use God's powerful weaponry to destroy addictions and false logic and everything that works its way up the ladder of the mind to pit itself against God's ways. Because we are led by the Spirit, and not by our flesh, we wrangle every loose thought that is unworthy, and fence it in. That fence is called *obedience to Christ*. Once everyone has had ample opportunity to align themselves with obedience, we'll be ready and willing to punish those who remain disobedient.

The facts are clear. Anyone who is convinced that he belongs to Christ should be able to take one look at the evidence of our lives and recognize immediately that we belong to Christ, too. Even if it seems like I'm always talking about myself, and specifically about my apostolic authority, I don't feel bad about that. I know it's coming from a right motive of trying to convince you that my message is God's message. It's all for your own good, not for my ego. It's to build you up, not to lord over you.

I'm not trying to scare you with my letters either. Some of you are saying, "Paul's letters are heavy-handed and give the impression of strength, but in person he's weak and what he says isn't worth much." We are serving notice on the people who think that: the way we talk in our letters is the way we're going to address you in person if things don't shape up fast. That's not a threat, it's a promise.

We *do not* consider ourselves to be in harmony with these so-called ministers who always talk about how great they are. They're birds of a feather who judge themselves only against themselves, rather than against God's unbiased standard. Not smart.

We're not going to brag on ourselves like that. We're simply going to continue to articulate the truth of the situation, which is that God has given us a significant sphere of authority, and you're in it! That's not bragging; those are just the cold, hard facts. We're not being presumptuous in asserting our authority over you. We're the ones who brought you the Gospel of Christ. You're our responsibility. And we've never tried to take credit for the work other people are doing. We just preach the Gospel with a confidence that as your faith grows, our sphere of influence grows as well, and we become better positioned to preach the Gospel in yet unreached areas. Then we won't be taking credit for anyone else's work there either. Jeremiah said it, "Whoever brags should only brag on what the Lord has done." You don't make the grade by telling everybody what a great job you're doing. You make the grade when *God* says you're doing a great job.

11 Okay, since you're so intent on accepting these fools based on their bragging, I guess I'll have to get foolish for a minute and brag on myself, too. Is that okay with you? Is that what it's come to? Well let's do it.

(Before I start bragging on myself, just know that the only reason I'm doing this is because I would do anything to convince you that *we* carry the Lord's message, and these fools don't. I'm jealous for you with a godly jealousy. You haven't really perceived the relationship here accurately. I'm not trying to court you; I'm the father of the bride. You are my daughter in the faith, and I am doing my best to keep my obligation to the Groom, Christ, to present Him with a pure virgin on His wedding day. But I'm afraid that somehow, just like Eve was deceived by the serpent's cunning ways, you're going to be tricked into rejecting the pure and simple truth of Christ. I know you're way too quick to accept teachings that are contrary to what we gave you: a jesus that's not Jesus, a spirit that's not the Spirit, and a gospel that's not the Gospel. I wouldn't have any problem stacking my credentials up against any apostle you want. Okay, I may not be the best speaker, but I know what I know, and it's a lot more than what these guys think they know. We've made that crystal clear on many occasions. Am I a terrible person for preaching the Gospel to you without charging you a fee? I was just being humble in order to clear the path to God for you. Meanwhile I had to rob the other churches to fund the mission to reach you. And when I was there with you, I didn't impose upon you when I needed something. The brothers from Macedonia met all my needs when they came. I have always ensured that I wouldn't be a bother to you, and I'll continue to act in that way. No sir, as surely as I carry the truth of Christ, nobody in Corinth and the surrounding regions is going to stop this little brag-fest. Why am I going to brag? Because I don't love you? Just the opposite. But I'm going to keep doing what I do, so that these bragging ministers won't be able to seize on the opportunity to elevate themselves to our level like they're hoping to. They are false apostles who are doing deceitful works. They have to be chameleons in order to claim to be the King's apostles. Not surprising. Satan transforms himself into an angel of light. It's not any more impressive for his servants to transform into servants of righteousness. In the end they'll receive justice for what they're doing.)

So here goes. Foolish talk and bragging. Let me reiterate that I'm only doing this to make a point. I would never say these things in earnest just to draw attention to myself. But since you like to hear all these fools feed their carnality by bragging about themselves, let me give it a try, too. I mean, you're willing to be re-enslaved, you're willing to throw your money at worthless drivel, you'll let them take advantage of you, you'll let them strut their stuff, and you'll let them slap you in the face! You're so wise! And I'm so ashamed that I can't be more like them! (Am I making the sarcasm obvious enough?) Anyway, let's give it a go. However audacious they are, let me be that audacious for a minute.

These guys are Hebrews by birth? And you think that gives them a leg up? Well, I was born a Hebrew, too. They've proven themselves Israelites by keeping all the customs? So have I. They're heirs of the promise to Abraham? So am I. They're servants to the King? If I'm being a foolish braggart right now, let me just say that I'm way more of a servant than they are. I've done much more work for the Lord. I've taken many more beatings for His sake. I've been imprisoned more frequently. I've faced death repeatedly. On five different occasions I received 39 lashes of the whip. Three times I was beaten with clubs. Once I was stoned, three times shipwrecked, one time in dire straits on the open sea for a whole 24 hours. Travelling constantly, I've faced danger at almost every turn. I've nearly drowned in rivers. I've been robbed. I've been targeted for persecution from both Jews and Gentiles. I've encountered dangerous situations in the cities, in the country, and at sea. I've also had dangerous encounters with the fake Christians. I've worked to the point of exhaustion, often going without sleep. I've been hungry and thirsty, even fasting long periods, often not by my own choice. I've been without proper clothing, causing me to be chilled to the bone.

If all that isn't enough, every day I deal with the concern I have for all of the churches. Who among you ever becomes weak without me also being weakened? Who is made to stumble in the faith without me feeling the burn of righteous indignation?

If I'm going to brag, I'm going to brag about the multi-faceted weakness I endure. Once when I was in Damascus, the governor under King Aretas put the entire city under military guard in order to arrest me. But I was put in a basket and let down out of a window in the city wall. That's how I escaped him. Our God and Father of the Lord Jesus Christ knows what I'm telling you is 100% true. Praise Him forever!

12 I feel like this foolish bragging is not going to do any good, but I'm on a roll now, so I'm gonna keep going. Here's something else you'll probably be impressed by: visions and revelations from the Lord. I know a man, a Christian man, who 14 years ago was caught up to the third heaven. Whether that was an out-of-body experience or whether his whole body was transported, I don't know. God knows. But what I do know is that this man was caught up to paradise and heard things nobody has permission to speak about. And he couldn't put it into words even if he wanted to.

(Do you understand that this man I'm talking about is actually me? I don't even want to say "I" because I have such a hard time drawing attention to myself like that. But it *was* an experience of significant importance, and in terms of a ministry résumé, it's the kind of thing that puts mine on the top of the stack. But, see, I just don't think like that. I don't think in terms of a revelatory vision giving me some kind of higher status. But since you do, there you have it. Add it to the list. It happened.)

And since it happened, since all these things happened, since I do have such a high rank among God's servants, it's not far-fetched to think I could become conceited about it. In fact, I probably would have, if not for this thorn in the flesh. I was given this messenger from Satan to beat me down and humiliate me so I would never be able to put myself up on a pedestal. I begged the Lord three times that this blasted thing would go away. But He just said, "My grace is all you need. The strength that I supply can only fill the tank of a weak person." So you'd better believe I'll take this frail, weak body of mine, if the trade-off is the joy and privilege of wielding the power of Christ! Aches and pains? Bring 'em on! Insults and criticisms? Bring 'em on! Mistreatment and persecution? Bring 'em on! The anguish of disastrous circumstances? For the sake of my King ... Bring! It! On! When I'm weak, He gets to be strong.

Okay, are you happy now? I've made a fool of myself by talking about all the things I've done for the Lord's sake, and the things He's done to make me a ranking apostle. Have I garnered your favor now that you see how much more impressive my résumé is than theirs? Ugh. I feel dirty. You should have been the ones commending me instead of me being forced to commend myself. Clearly the signs of an apostle were demonstrated before your very eyes, a sustained barrage of miracles, signs, and wonders. Come up with one way that I did less to prove myself in Corinth than in any of the other churches? Oh, that's right, I refused to take your money! Well *ex-cuuuuuuse* me!

Now this will be my third visit coming up. And I won't be an imposition on you this time either. I'm not after your stuff; I'm after your souls. Children don't save up for their parents; parents save up for their children. I'm more than willing to use my resources, as well as my time and energy, to ensure you stay on track, although it seems the more I love you, the less you love me. I've never been a burden to you. Would you really accuse me of tricking and entrapping you? Did I take advantage of you via any of the emissaries I sent? I pushed for Titus to go to you, and I sent the other brother with him. Titus never took advantage of you, did he? Hasn't he always displayed the same spirit and purpose I have?

Do you think we're saying all of this stuff merely in self-defense. No, dear friends, it's much more than that. Before God in Christ I tell you that we're defending ourselves in order to achieve the much more important goal of building you up in the faith to the place where you need to be. My fear is that when I get there, I won't like what I see, and if that's the case, you won't like what you see out of me either. I'm afraid I'll find pointless disputes and discord, zealous defense of nothingness, anger boiling up and exploding, sleazy politics, character assassination, secret smear campaigns, arrogance, and chaos. And I hope I won't be humiliated in God's sight by finding that there are still many who have not repented of the sins we've already addressed: shameless immorality, unauthorized sexual relationships, unrestrained lustfulness. I would be so grieved.

13 This will be my third visit. "Let every word be confirmed by two or three witnesses," the Scripture says. I told you when I was there last time, and I'm telling you again now: to all those who were in sin before, and everybody else for that matter, when I come this time I will not hold back if things haven't changed. You wanted proof that Christ speaks through me? Well you'll get it. He's not timid in His approach. He works powerfully among you. He was weak when He went to the cross, but the fact that He's alive now demonstrates His great power. And we're physically weak because of our dedication to Him, but when we get there, we'll be bringing that same resurrection power He has.

So examine yourselves to see if you're really in the faith. Put yourself through the paces and see if the genuineness of your faith can be proven. If King Jesus lives in you, don't you know it? Unless you don't actually pass the test. But I trust you can plainly see that we do pass the test. And we're praying that you won't continue to do wrong by refusing to heed this message. We would rather you do what's right and us look like we're unwilling to be harsh, than for you to do wrong and us have to prove that we can be harsh. We're happy for you to be strong and us to look weak. But we can't do anything that doesn't align with the Truth. So, I'm writing these things, from a distance, so that when I get there I won't have to use the authority the Lord has given me to be severe with you. Of course, if I do, it will only be to build you up, not to tear you down. *Lord, make them complete, everything You want them to be.*

Well, we've come to the end, friends. We'll say goodbye. Become what you ought to be. Encourage and comfort one another. Live with a unified purpose. Keep the peace. And the God of love and peace will be with you.

Greet each other in the love of God. All of God's holy people send their greetings.

May the love of Father God, the grace of the Lord Jesus Christ, and the intimate fellowship of the Holy Spirit be with you all. Amen.

Discussion Questions

WEEK 16: 2 Corinthians 1-7

- Toward the end of Chapter 1 and the beginning of Chapter 2, we learn that Paul wanted to visit the Corinthians, but was forced to write a previous letter instead. What can you tell about the contents of that letter, and Paul's general feelings toward the Corinthian church, at the time he wrote that letter and at the time he wrote this one?

- The opening of Chapter 3 is a pretty good example of what seems to be Paul's primary reason for writing this letter. Discuss.

- What does Chapter 4 reveal about the nature of true Christianity?

- Throughout the letter we see what seems to be a bit of contradiction in Paul's attitude toward the Corinthians, displeased with them one minute (e.g., Ch. 6) and thrilled with them the next (e.g., Ch. 7). How might these apparent contradictions be explained in a way that makes sense?

WEEK 17: 2 Corinthians 8-13

- Paul challenges the Corinthians in Chapters 8-9 to give liberally to those Christians who were in poverty. The Macedonians were poor themselves, and yet they gave until it hurt. What light does this shed on the current state of giving in Western Christendom?

- What are the powerful weapons of God that we use to destroy everything that pits itself against God's ways? (Chapter 10)

- Discuss the contrast between Paul's "fool" speech (Chapters 11-12) and the bragging of the false apostles he is defending himself against? What kinds of things do you look for today as the measure of a minister's value?

- Paul exhorts us to examine ourselves to see if we're really in the faith: "Put yourself through the paces and see if the genuineness of your faith can be proven." Discuss how we can do that, and then put it into practice this week.

THESSALONIANS

1 To the church of the Thessalonians, a group of people who belong to God our Father and the Lord Jesus Christ,

We pray you receive a full supply of Father God's grace and peace, which is poured out liberally by the Lord Jesus Christ.

We are constantly thanking God for you, bringing you up before Him when we pray. In our time with Father God, we are continually reminded of your faith-inspired actions, the work you put into demonstrating His love, and your steadiness, which comes from your hope in the Lord Jesus Christ.

Dear friends, it is clear to us, for two reasons, that God has chosen you to be His: 1) because we remember how confident you were in the Gospel message we preached, seeing as how the Holy Spirit confirmed it with miracle-working power; and 2) you saw what our lives were like when we were there, and you chose to imitate us and the Lord even though it meant you were forced to suffer persecution.

The joy from the Holy Spirit that you maintained in the face of that trouble made you a shining example for our brothers and sisters in Macedonia and southern Greece to follow. Indeed the Lord's message is being propelled beyond Macedonia and southern Greece; they're hearing your story everywhere. We don't even have to say anything when we visit someplace new. They're telling *us* about the lovely welcome you gave us, and how you turned away from worshipping idols and began to worship the one true living God. They say, "Those Thessalonians know Jesus, they know He's God's Son, they know He was raised from the dead, they know He's going to save us from the coming wrath, and they are waiting expectantly for Him to return from heaven."

2 Church, you know how profitable our visit together was. Even after we had suffered terrible treatment at Philippi, we were still willing to come preach the Gospel to you, and we faced opposition there as well. But we preached anyway, a straightforward presentation of the truth, with no ulterior motives. We don't preach to be liked, we preach to bring about change. We don't cater to people, we cater to God. He's the One who approved and entrusted us to carry the Gospel message, and He's the One who tests us to see if our hearts are in the right place. So we didn't preach feel-good sermons with warm fuzzy ideas. And we weren't making a pretense just to get money either. God knows that's the truth.

We also weren't there to receive accolades from you, or from anyone else for that matter. We could have pulled rank on some things and insisted that we be given the red carpet treatment befitting "apostles of Christ." But we didn't. We were the givers. Like a nursing mother adores and gladly provides for her child, we were there for you and you only. We grew so fond of you that we gave you more than just the Gospel message, we gave you a piece of ourselves. That's how much you meant to us. And as we preached God's good news, you have to remember, we worked so hard, day and night, so we could support ourselves, just so we wouldn't be a burden to you.

You saw how we were holy and righteous and above reproach in our interactions with all the people of faith, and God saw it, too. And we cheered you up and encouraged you and challenged you, all of you, as a father tries to help his children. And we did all of these things in the hope that you would walk in a manner worthy of the God who called you to advance His kingdom and experience His glory.

So we're always thanking God that you received His communiqué from us with open arms, believing it to be the true and trustworthy Word of God Himself. Because you believed, that Word has changed your lives. And it led you to follow in the footsteps of God's churches in Judea, suffering at the hands of your own neighbors just as they suffered at the hands of theirs. They killed the Lord Jesus, not to mention their own prophets, and now they're after us. They antagonize God with their hostile efforts to thwart us from evangelizing the Gentiles. Their sins have reached the point of no return, and the wrath of God has finally caught up with them.

We may be temporarily separated from you physically, but not spiritually and emotionally. We want to have another face-to-face visit now more than ever. We have wanted to come see you—I, Paul, have tried more than once—but Satan wrecked our plans. We want to see you because you're our pride and joy, and you give us an assurance that we will get to wear a glorious crown when the Lord Jesus returns and we get to be with Him!

3 When we were in Athens, we could hardly stand not being in contact with you. But since we thought it was best to stay isolated at that point, we did the next best thing: we sent Timothy to strengthen and encourage you. You know he's God's servant, and our brother, our coworker in spreading the good news of the risen King. We sent him because we wanted you to stay strong in the faith and not worry about all the trials we're enduring. You do know that persecution is our lot in life, don't you? In fact, we told you when we were there that we were going to suffer tribulation. And that's exactly what's happened.

At any rate, I couldn't stand not knowing whether you were still keeping the faith or whether you had proven our work fruitless by succumbing to the temptation of that wily scoundrel. So I sent Timothy to find out. But now that Timothy has returned with a good report, we are elated that your faith still stands strong. He says you are demonstrating God's love and remaining faithful to His commands. He says you're always remembering us and wanting to see us again. (And, of course, we want to see you, too.) So, even in the middle of this calamity we're in, we have a shot of energy knowing that you are standing firm in the Lord. We can't thank God enough for the joy your testimony has brought us. We intently pray night and day that we will get to see you again and give you what you need in order for your faith to operate at 100% efficiency.

May Father God and our Lord Jesus Christ pave the way for us to reunite. May the Lord cultivate your love for one another and for the world until it's bursting at the seams. (That's how we feel toward you.) And may God cement your hearts in place, blameless and holy before Him, so that you may revel in the coming of the Lord Jesus Christ, along with all the saints.

4 Finally, church, we're asking you, even strongly pushing you, in the Lord Jesus, to go the extra mile in living out all the teaching we've given you on how to please God. You're doing well with it, and we're saying: go even further. You know all the rules we relayed to you by the authority of the Lord Jesus, how it's God's will that you become more and more holy. At the most basic level that entails refusing to engage in sexually immoral behavior. You need to keep your body parts holy and honorable before God. Don't be controlled by wrong desires. That's what non-Christians do. You should never cheat or dishonor each other that way, because the Lord avenges all such wrongs, as we told you before. Church, God has not called you to impurity but to holiness. Anyone who rejects what we're saying here is not merely rejecting a man's opinion, but rather God's eternal standard of living, confirmed by the Holy Spirit He has given us.

Now I don't need to say anything to you about loving each other. God has taught you directly how important that is. And you've demonstrated His love, particularly toward all of our brothers and sisters in Macedonia. So we just say keep it up, and do even more!

Do your best to live above reproach. Mind your own business, work your own job, stay out of peoples' faces. If you behave yourselves, hopefully you'll be able to avoid trouble. If you are honorable in all your dealings with the people outside the church, you'll build a good reputation, and you'll have everything you need.

Now friends, I want you to be informed when it comes to Jesus' return and what it means for those who have already died. We don't have to grieve like the unbelievers who have no hope after death. We believe in *life* after death. The same God who brought Jesus back to life after He died will bring all of His deceased followers back to life, too!

Hear what the Lord has said, Church: Those of us who are still alive when Jesus returns will not have any advantage over those who have already died. Here's what will happen. The Lord Himself will come down out of the skies and shout out His glorious command, at which point the archangel will sound the trumpet of God. In response, those Christians who have died will be resurrected. That happens first. Then *all* of Jesus' followers—the ones who are still alive when He comes *and* the newly resurrected ones—will be snatched up together to take our place in the clouds. There, in the air, we will meet the Lord, and we will be with Him from that point on, forever. So, keep encouraging each other by recounting this message.

5 Regarding the exact year, month, day, and time, I don't need to spell all that out, church. You know full well that the Day of the Lord comes as a thief in the night. As soon as they begin to feel safe and secure in the rationalizing of their sin, catastrophic devastation ensues as suddenly and as forcefully as a pregnant woman's contractions. And there's no escaping it at that point. But you're not in the dark, so you don't need to worry about this thief. You won't be destroyed on the Day the Lord comes, because you are children of light and children of the day.

Since we're not night-people and darkness-people, let's not fall asleep at the wheel, as others do. Let's be sober and keep a watchful eye out. People who dull their senses by getting drunk, and sleep instead of being alert, do so at night. But we are people of the day, so let's do things fitting for daytime: staying sober and staying alert. Guard your hearts with the armor of faith and love, and guard your minds with the helmet of the hope of salvation. The wrath that God will be unleashing is earmarked for the world, not for us. Instead, He's preserving us for the culmination of our salvation through our Lord Jesus Christ. He died so we could live with Him forever. Whether or not we die before He returns doesn't change that fact.

So, continue building each other up and encouraging one another, as I know you're already doing. And pay attention to your church leadership, when they affirm you and when they warn you. They're working hard for you, so think highly of them, always viewing them through the eyes of love. And be at peace.

Now, brothers and sisters, here are some things to remember to do. Gently correct those who are out of order. Encourage those who are down. Support those who are weak. Be patient with everyone. Two wrongs don't make a right; make sure that second, retaliatory wrong never happens. Everyone should always be doing right by each other and by those in the world. Maintain the joy of the Lord at all times. Don't stop praying. Give God thanks in the middle of every situation; He allows all of life's mountains and valleys to shape you into who He wants you to be in Christ Jesus. Don't do anything that would keep the Spirit from having free reign in your lives. Don't write off prophetic words, but test them all, and hold onto what is good. And stay away from every variety of evil.

Now may the God of Peace Himself make you completely holy. And may your spirit, soul, and body be kept blameless until the coming of our Lord Jesus Christ. He's the One who called you; He'll accomplish the work.

Friends, pray for us.

Greet one another in God's love.

In the name of the Lord, I insist that you read this letter to everyone in the church.

May the grace of the Lord Jesus Christ be with you always.

Love,
Paul, along with Silas and Timothy

1 To the church of the Thessalonians, the property of God our Father and the Lord Jesus Christ,

We're sending you another dose of God's grace and peace, in the name of the Lord Jesus Christ.

We're obliged to continually thank God for you, church. It's totally appropriate for us to do so, because your faith keeps growing by leaps and bounds, and the love you show to each other is extraordinary.

We keep telling all of God's churches about your persistent patience and faith through the many persecutions and tribulations you're enduring. The fact that you're not giving up on God in spite of all the difficulties is the evidence that He has judged you worthy to receive what you're suffering for: His Kingdom.

God's justice demands that He crush those who are crushing you and give rest to you who are burdened for His sake. He will do just that when He returns. Count on it! He will appear in the skies in a blazing inferno, with His powerful angel army right behind Him. Then He will take vengeance on everyone who never cared about God, those who don't put the Good News of Jesus Christ into practice by obeying Him as Master. When He comes in that Day, He will punish them with everlasting destruction. They will be forever separated from the presence of God and from the glory of His power. But in His holy people He will be glorified. Everyone who trusts in Him will praise and adore Him forever. And you'll be part of this celebration, all because you believed the message that we preached to you.

So we keep praying for you, that God will enable you to be counted worthy of His calling and that He will empower you to perform all the good deeds your faith is giving you the desire to do. May God's grace cause the name of the Lord Jesus Christ to be glorified in you and you to be glorified in Him.

2 Now church, we need to set the record straight about when Jesus will return and gather us up to be with Him. Don't get all riled up by people who claim that the Day of the Lord has already come. There's no basis for such an alarming report, so don't let anybody trick you into believing it under any circumstances, even if they claim to have insight from the Spirit or from the Word or from a letter that we supposedly wrote.

That Day won't come until after the great apostasy has commenced and the antagonist is revealed—the man of lawlessness, the child of hell. He will elevate himself above all other idols so that he alone is worshipped. And he will directly oppose the true God by sitting in the Most Holy Place of His Temple and proclaiming himself to be god.

Don't you remember I told you these things when I was with you? And you also know what's holding him back right now. He can't be put in power too early. He has to wait for his time. Most people don't even notice that the spirit of lawlessness is already at work right now. It will remain under the radar until the One who keeps it from reaching the boiling point steps aside. Then evil will be able to go unchecked.

That's when the man of lawlessness will appear. He has to have his own counterfeit "coming" before the Lord appears in His authentic coming. Satan is the event planner for the counterfeit coming. It's his power that the antagonist will use to display all sorts of counterfeit signs and wonders. The man of lawlessness will use his wickedness to deceive all those who are headed toward death. They will be sucked in by it because they didn't love the truth and latch onto it while they had the chance, so they could be saved. That's why God will send them a strong delusion, so that they will believe the lie. When the Lord Jesus returns in magnificent splendor, He will bring the antagonist's reign to an end and kill him with breath from His mouth, and all those who ignored the truth and instead chose to enjoy the temporary pleasures of sin will be condemned.

But not you, brothers and sisters! You are dearly loved by the Lord. We owe God a debt of thanks for you, because He chose you right up front to be saved, through sanctification by the Spirit and through your belief in the truth. He opened your eyes to that truth when we first preached the Gospel to you, and through it the glory of the Lord Jesus Christ will become your own prized possession. So church, stand firm and hold onto all of the doctrines you were taught—the ones we shared with you face to face and the ones we wrote to you about.

Now, may our Lord Jesus Christ Himself, and Father God, who loves us and never stops comforting us, and who has given us a good hope by His grace, comfort your hearts and substantiate every good thing you say and do.

3 Finally, friends, pray for us. Pray that the message of Jesus will spread rapidly and that those who hear it will hold it dear, just as you did. And pray that God will rescue us from unreasonable and wicked men. Not everybody has the faith, but the Lord is faithful to us. And He will give you strength and protect you from the evil one. We are confident in the Lord that you are doing and will continue to do everything we've told you to do. Now may the Lord remove every hindrance from receiving God's love and Christ's patience into your hearts.

Church, we insist, in the name of our Lord Jesus Christ, that you break ties with every so-called brother who is consistently out of order or does not follow the ordinances we laid out for you. You all know that you are to follow our example and teachings. We were not out of order when we were there with you. We didn't even presume to take free meals from you. We worked side jobs, day and night, just so we wouldn't be a burden to you, not because we didn't have the right to expect you to give us room and board, but simply to make ourselves examples that you could follow. Because when we were there, we told you that people who don't work don't eat. So we made sure we practiced what we preached.

But we're hearing that some folks in your congregation *are* out of order. They won't work a job, but they have no problem working the gossip train and other useless pursuits. These people need to hear what we're saying right now: work an honest living and eat what you provide for yourself, and other than that, keep your mouth shut.

As for everyone else, don't get tired of doing good. If anyone chooses not to obey the instructions we've written in this letter, take note of that person, and stop hanging out with him, so that he'll feel the shame of his poor choice. Don't totally write him off as a hostile apostate though. Just warn him honestly, as a brother who's missed the mark.

Now may the Lord of Peace Himself always give you peace in every circumstance. *Lord, be with them all.*

This is Paul signing off in my own handwriting, which is something I like to do in all my letters as a sign of authenticity. May the grace of our Lord Jesus Christ be with you all. Amen.

Love,
Paul, along with Silas and Timothy

Discussion Questions

WEEK 18: 1 Thessalonians & 2 Thessalonians

- Both letters to the Thessalonians are initiated by an overwhelming feeling of thanks Paul and his coworkers have because of the faithfulness of the church. How do they know the Thessalonians' faith is genuine (1Th 1)? How might others know your faith is genuine?

- Another reason Paul wrote these letters was to answer the questions the Thessalonians had, in particular about the end times. What question was he answering in the first letter (1Th 4)? What question was he answering in the second letter (2Th 2)?

- Chapter 2 of 2 Thessalonians indicates that a great apostasy or turning away will occur before the Lord returns. Do you see signs of that in today's world? What steps should we be taking to ensure we are not the ones who will turn away?

- What are some of the other instructions given in these letters?

THE **FIRST** LETTER FROM
PETER

1 To the saints dispersed all over Turkey,

You've been chosen by the Father to be cleansed by the blood of the Son and sanctified by the Spirit. He did this even though He knew that you in no way deserved such a blessing. Nevertheless, you are now empowered to live a life of obedience to Him! And it is my sincere pleasure to pronounce upon you a great increase of grace and peace.

Let me begin by praising God, the Father of our Lord Jesus Christ. Out of the abundance of His mercy He has conceived us by His Spirit, so that we could be born again through Jesus' resurrection from the dead. Now we are living a new life full of a hope that cannot fail. We have an assurance of an eternal inheritance in heaven that can't decompose or diminish in purity. And God is holding us in the palm of His hand, keeping us on track, through our faith, for the final realization of our salvation at the last Day.

I know you're ecstatic about this, even though recently you've had to endure such agonizing trials in pursuit of that reward. Consider it a great honor that God has allowed you to suffer this kind of persecution for His sake. And, oh, what a test! You've gone through the fire for Jesus, and you're still standing. Now we *all* know that you are practicing the genuine faith, pure as gold. Even though you've never seen Jesus, you believe in Him as if you had, and you have an excitement about your final destiny of salvation and glory that can't even be put into words.

The Holy Spirit impressed the concept of salvation upon the prophets that came before us, and they always wondered when and how God would finally make it a reality. They knew that a Messiah would come, that He would suffer, and that He would usher in something glorious. They also knew that they would be beneficiaries of the grace He would achieve, even though they wouldn't physically see it happen. When they prophesied about Him, they knew they were saying those things to us and for us, and yet what they saw was only a hazy picture of what was to come. Even the angels have been excited to see how the plan would all come together.

Since we are so privileged to be the ones who have heard the Gospel and received the Holy Spirit, it's so important that we live soberly, maintaining a mindset of diligence, resting in the One who will bring us into the fullness of His grace when He appears to us in person. So be obedient children. Don't let yourself continue to conform to the desires and behavior patterns that you practiced before you saw the light. The God who has called you to Himself is set apart and totally *other*. Which means you, too, must be set apart and totally *other*, in order to commune with Him. The Scripture said it: "Be holy because I am holy."

Now, if you call God your Father, then live your life in a way that honors that Father-son relationship, going about your business with reverent fear. After all, He is going to judge each and every one of us according to what we do. Remember that the ransom God used to buy you out of the worthless life your ancestors passed down to you wasn't mere earthly treasures like silver and gold. No, it was the battered body of Jesus and the blood that poured from His gaping wounds that secured our freedom from the guilt and power of sin. He was our perfect, sacrificial Lamb, and His act of redemption and reconciliation was ordained by God before the foundation of the world was laid. Now that act has materialized, and it applies directly to you in the present time. Those who believe in God through Jesus have a secure faith and hope anchored in His glorious resurrection from the dead.

Since your obedience to the truth has purified your hearts, use those pure hearts to love your brothers and sisters in the Lord fervently. The eternal Word of God was the seed that developed in your spirit, eventually leading you to be born again. This wasn't a natural process, susceptible to death or defect; this was a process of the Spirit. "People are like grass, and their accomplishments are like a flower. The grass turns brown, and the flower soon disappears. But what the Lord speaks into your life is not like that. It lives on forever." And indeed the Lord did speak salvation into your life when you heard and believed the Gospel.

2 So, don't lose that desire for the pure milk of the Word that you had when you were spiritual newborns. If you feel yourself bent toward wickedness, deceitfulness, or jealousy, kick those things to the curb. Don't be hypocrites either, and don't defame others. Of course, I'm saying all these things with the assumption that you *have* actually tasted the grace of God. Perhaps you're even asking yourself whether you truly have experienced His grace. Well, follow me for a minute.

Imagine the Messiah is a stone. It's actually not hard to imagine, because that's exactly how the psalmist described Him: "From now on, the Stone that the builders rejected will function as the Primary Cornerstone." Now, in this statement we see two responses to the Stone. Some of the people who come across the Stone see Him as One to be rejected; others see Him as One to be aligned with. Isaiah says the same thing. To some He is "The Primary Cornerstone whom I, the Lord, am laying in Zion, precious and chosen for this very purpose. Whoever believes in Him will have no cause for shame." But to others He is "A Stone that makes them stumble, and a Rock that offends them." See, to those who believe, He is precious, but to those who are disobedient, He destines them to stumble. It's quite simple really. You have, no doubt, encountered this Stone. Well, is He tripping you up, or is He causing you to come into alignment with Him?

Friends, I urge you to come to Him, this precious Stone, chosen by God, who lives and breathes. When you do, you, too, become a living, breathing stone, and the Father will spread His mortar all over you and place you right in among all the other stones. He's building us up into a house that His Spirit can inhabit. And He's building us up as His new priesthood, holy and set apart, whose job it is to sacrifice our own wills and desires in favor of His. Jesus empowers us to do just that.

Yes, you are the people of His choosing, a company of royal priests, a holy tribe. And you have been called out of darkness into His marvelous light so you can shout His praises. You who were once not even considered a people-group are now the very people of God. You who once knew no mercy have now been shown abundant mercy.

Friends, I'm begging you, as spiritual foreigners living in a natural world, steer clear of the passions of the flesh, lusts that wear down the defenses of the soul. Always conduct yourself with integrity among unbelievers, so that even if they speak against you now, they'll have no choice but to recant and testify to your fidelity on Judgment Day.

Therefore, for the Lord's sake, submit to every form of authority on earth that you find yourself placed under. That would include kings and presidents, senators and governors, police forces and judges, employers, church leaders, and on and on. God's will is that you keep yourself squeaky clean in the eyes of the world so that there's no chance you could ever lead anyone to think poorly of the God you represent. Christian freedom is in no way a license to behave badly toward others. After all, you may be free from sin, but you're still enslaved to the Lord Jesus. Ascribe value to all humanity, demonstrate the love of God to everyone in the Christian community, maintain a reverent fear of God, and pay honor to the head of state.

Employees, treat your bosses with respect, and maintain a submissive spirit toward them. Do this whether they are good to you or they mistreat you. God always receives glory when somebody who is being mistreated by an authority chooses to take the high road in every circumstance and endure suffering for His sake. Now, I'm not talking about taking a beating for something you actually did wrong. But patiently enduring harsh and unjust treatment when you've done nothing wrong proves that you are full of God's grace. And you were called to follow in Christ's footsteps with respect to suffering injustice. "He never once sinned, nor did He ever speak anything deceitful." When He was abused, He didn't lash out in return. He didn't even threaten His abusers with judgment, but simply yielded Himself to the Father, knowing that His righteous judgment would be the final say. At the end of His torturous trial, there He was, hanging on the tree, having taken our sins upon His own body. The stripes on His back have secured our healing, and the blood that drained out of Him has made a way for us to live righteously. We who were once like wandering sheep have been found by the Shepherd, and He now guards our souls.

3 While I'm on this topic of submitting to authority, wives, God has given you your husbands to be your spiritual leaders. Ideally, they should take that role seriously, submitting themselves to God in order to be good and godly servant-leaders within the home. But even if they're derelict in this duty and don't follow the Lord, continue to maintain a submissive spirit toward them. That way they may be won over by your purity and reverent behavior. Your outer appearance (your clothes, your jewelry, and your hairstyle) isn't nearly as important as your inner appearance. Keeping a gentle and quiet spirit will give you a beauty that won't diminish with age, and *that* is precious to God. This is the way the saintly women of the past treated their husbands. Take Sarah, for instance, who obeyed Abraham and called him *lord*. See, you are spiritual descendants of Sarah if you treat your husbands with respect and leave the rest in God's hands.

On the other hand, husbands, you need to place value on your wives. Just because they're weaker than you doesn't give you the right to be domineering. You are in this thing together, and you have jointly inherited a life of vibrancy by God's grace.

So treat them right. That way your prayers will not be hindered.

And now, to everyone, I say *be of one mind.* Have compassion on others, recognizing that they're human just like you. Love your Christian brothers and sisters as if they're your biological siblings. And be tender and kind to each other. If someone berates you or makes trouble for you, don't turn right around and berate and make trouble for them. Rather, invoke blessing on them, because you know you are heirs to blessing. Heed this word from David: "If you want your life to be good, speak no evil and don't be deceitful. Turn away from what's wrong and do what's right. Earnestly endeavor to find peace. For the Lord hears every prayer and sees every sacrifice of the righteous. But He sets His face against those who do evil."

Who's going to hurt you if you make it your goal to always do right? And even if you do have to endure suffering because of your devotion to the cause of righteousness, that would be an eternal blessing to you. So, "don't be worried or afraid of such threats." Instead, be sure that you've set God up as the Lord over your heart, and always be ready to explain to people how your commitment to Jesus gives you an unshakeable hope. Speak with them gently, however, in reverent deference to the purposes of God's Spirit in that moment. That way your conscience will remain clear, and if they run a smear campaign against you, it will be to their own disgrace.

If God wills that you suffer for doing good, how much better is that than to avoid suffering by doing evil? Even Jesus suffered, and we know He only did what was good. His suffering was the remedy for our sins. The Righteous One gave Himself for us, the unrighteous. He paved the way for us to be reconciled to God, dying in His flesh, but being raised to new life by the Spirit. This message of Christ condemns all those of the previous generations who were disobedient. God was patient with these self-serving people as Noah built the ark, but eventually He said, "Enough is enough," and the unrighteous met their fate of eternal imprisonment, while those eight faithful people were saved. Likewise, God is still patient today, and He's still in the business of saving people. When we are baptized, we're following the pattern, established in Noah's day, of salvation through water. This act of obedience doesn't literally remove the filth of our sin, rather baptism is the acting out of our faith in God to wash our consciences clean. All of this is only made possible by the resurrection of Jesus Christ, who ascended to heaven and assumed all of the authority of the Father. Now every angel and demon is subject to Him.

4 So, if Christ suffered physical pain, you need to prepare yourselves to suffer as well. If you're able to suffer for Him in this way, then you'll know you've left sin in the rearview mirror. You won't be spending the rest of your life following your own carnal desires, but you'll rather be fully devoted to God's will. You spent more than enough time in your former life doing all the heathen things that heathens do—unrestrained sexual immorality, craving all the things that are off limits, drunkenness and the riotous nightlife that follows it, and the repulsive practice of idolatry. The people who live life with that kind of reckless abandon are confused as to why you no longer act the same way. And now they slander you without cause. Don't worry, the time will come when they will stand before the One who judges the living and the dead. (See, we who have received the Gospel are not the only ones who will be saved on that Day. That same Gospel is going out to those saints who have already died, bringing them the comfort of salvation. They may have received man's judgment of physical death, but when that Day comes, they will receive the Spirit's judgment of eternal life right along with us.)

Church, the end of the world is right around the corner. So be calm and collected in your spirit, and be sober in your approach to prayer. Most of all, love each other ardently, for "love overcomes so many sins." Open up your homes and your hearts to each other, and resist the urge to take offense and secretly complain about it.

Every one of you has received a spiritual gift. Share those gifts with each other, bearing in mind that their purpose is not for you to stroke your own ego, but for His love and encouragement to increase. If you minister to God's people, simply do it according to the ability God has given you, no more and no less. If you address the congregation, speak as the oracle of God. We're talking about the Creator of the universe speaking through you! Knowing this should make you as bold and confident as a lion toward the people, yet as humble and submissive as a trained dog toward God. In all of these things, let your primary aim be the ever-increasing glory of God through Jesus Christ. All glory and power flow from Him and back to Him. Amen and amen!

Dear friends, don't be surprised when you find yourself being heated to the melting point. Such trials are necessary to bring all of the impurities to the surface. So take joy in the fact that you get to suffer as Christ suffered. In the end, when the fullness of His glory is poured out, you'll be elated. To be taunted for the sake of living out true Christianity is to attain blessing. Faithfulness in that kind of situation is a sure sign that God's Spirit and God's glory rest on you. To the degree that God is blasphemed by them, He is glorified through you. To be clear, I'm not talking about suffering the due punishment for murder, robbery, or any other kind of crime. I'm not even talking about suffering the adverse consequence of meddling in other people's business. That kind of suffering should, of course, never be heard of among you. But if you suffer persecution on account of your Christian faith, don't be ashamed, but give glory to God. When God sets His mind to executing judgment, He starts with His own people, and then moves on to everyone else. And that time has begun. We can expect to feel Him turn up the heat on us, so that we may be found pure on the last Day. "And if it's only with such difficulty that we, the righteous, are saved, what hope do the unrighteous have?" Therefore, be fully submitted to God your Creator, knowing that His will for you is best, even if that will is that you should suffer persecution for His sake.

5 Now, to all the elders over the various churches, please receive these words and put them into practice. (Just for context, I'm an elder, too; I witnessed Christ's suffering firsthand; and I can assure you I'll be invited to the party when the glory of God is revealed.) Shepherd well the flock that God has given you. Serve them as overseers, not as dictators, not out of a sense of duty, but out of a heart surrendered to the will of God. Don't get into ministry with aspirations of fame and fortune. Only enter into this noble profession if you know that God has called you to it and you're willing to eagerly follow Him wherever He leads, serving as an example to those under your authority. If you will lead in this way, when the Chief Shepherd appears, you'll receive a crown of glory that will gleam brightly forever.

To those who are younger, submit yourselves to your elders. In fact, all of you should maintain submissive and humble spirits, showing deference to one another. For "God resists the proud, but gives grace to the humble." Therefore, truly humble yourselves in your own minds, and in the sight of God. If you don't exalt yourself, He will have the opportunity to exalt you, and that's a much better outcome. Don't worry about what time or season you will see breakthrough. God cares about you more than you could ever imagine. Trust Him. You can be sure that He only ever does what's best for you.

Be sober and stay on guard at all times, Church! The devil is on the hunt, and your souls are his prey. He roars like a lion, and indeed he is an able foe who can pounce on you and have your bones licked clean before you even know what's happened. But praise God, we do have a great defense against him. It's called steadfastly clinging to the faith, keeping your sights set on Jesus every step of the way. If you maintain this kind of vigilance, you'll be able to resist that scoundrel. And be encouraged, Christians all over the world are going through the same kind of suffering you are. We're all going to get there, by God's grace. He has called us into His eternal glory by Christ Jesus. After your temporary suffering is over, you'll realize that He's making you complete, stable, strong, and grounded. To Him be all glory and power forever and ever. Amen.

I've been dictating this letter to our faithful brother, Silas, who was gracious to write it all out. I know it's been brief, but I trust that the crux of it has really hit home, which is simply this: You are standing firm in the grace of God; keep it up!

The Christian community here in this modern-day Babylon sends its greetings. In particular, so does Mark, my son in the faith.

Greet each other in the love of God. Peace be with everyone who is in Christ. Amen.

Your servant-leader,
Peter, an apostle of Jesus Christ

Discussion Questions

WEEK 19: 1 Peter

- Peter describes Jesus as a Stone who lives and breathes. Is this Stone tripping you up or causing you to come into alignment with Him? If you feel yourself coming into alignment with Him, take a moment and praise God! If you feel convicted that you are consistently pushing back against God and His ways, take this opportunity to cry out in repentance and allow Him to tenderize your heart.

- Peter tells us to "always be ready to explain to people how your commitment to Jesus gives you an unshakeable hope" (Chapter 3). Let's put this into practice. Each participant, explain the Gospel of Jesus Christ in your own words. Help each other grow in the skill of verbally defending the faith.

- Suffering persecution for the faith is a theme that runs throughout the letter. Is this something you've ever had to endure? Have you ever thought ahead to a time when you might need to be prepared for such persecution?

- Peter advises us not to "worry about what time or season we should see breakthrough" (Chapter 5). Are you looking for a dream to be fulfilled? Take a moment to hand over the timing of that to God in complete trust.

THE SECOND LETTER FROM
PETER

1 To all those who have laid claim to the precious faith that is only made possible by the righteousness of our God and Savior, Jesus Christ,

May you ever increase in the grace and peace that comes from knowing God and allowing Jesus to be the Master of your life. His divine power surges through us, giving us the ability to live godly lives full of virtue and glory. The more we come to know God, the better we get at avoiding worldly cravings and the death and decay they lead to. Think about the indescribably magnificent promises He has made to us. He actually wants us to be so unified with Him that His divine nature is at work in us!

For this very reason, be as diligent as you can to build layer upon layer of His character into your life. We start with faith. To that we add a lifestyle marked by virtuous actions. To that we add a mind full of godly wisdom and knowledge. Then we begin to notice that we are in full control of ourselves. After conquering our passions in this way, we should be able to withstand the tough times without losing focus on our mission. Having gone this far, surely we will prove a high degree of reverence and piety toward God. To these qualities we should add kindness. And at the end of it all, we must put on the type of love only God can supply. Friends, if you have all of these things, you'll become everything God wants you to be and accomplish everything He wants you to accomplish. But if you're not developing in these areas, then you're not keeping your sights set on the higher purpose, you've forgotten the sinful state you were saved out of, and you're reverting back to spiritual blindness. So, Church, don't let your intensity for pursuing God and His ways wane. Do everything you know to do to confirm the sovereign choice God made when He called you. If you keep moving forward in these things, you won't lose your footing. This is the *way* in which we will one day enter the kingdom of our Lord and Savior Jesus Christ.

Given the weightiness of everything I just said, it's totally appropriate for me to continually remind you of these things, even though I know you already know the drill. I'm convinced it's the right thing to do to keep stimulating your minds and hearts toward this end. After all, the Lord has revealed to me that I won't be around much longer. But, I'm going to make sure that you even have reminders when I'm dead and gone.

Listen, people. When we first explained to you how Jesus had come, how He was the promised Messiah, and how He should be the Lord of your lives, we weren't spinning some fairy tale. We were actual eyewitnesses to His majesty! I'm thinking particularly of the time when we went up the holy mountain with Him, and the Father spoke honor and glory over Him from heaven, saying, "This is My Son. I love Him, and I am very pleased with Him." And when we told you these things, we confirmed them with a demonstration of His power!

On top of that, we have the words of the prophets, which have now been confirmed in the person of Jesus Christ! You need to pay attention to these words. They serve as a light in the darkness. Wasn't the message of Jesus like the sun rising in your hearts? The prophecies that Jesus fulfilled will keep us encouraged until that last Day dawns and our hearts are filled to capacity. So, keep this in mind: no biblical prophecy is up for nuanced interpretation; not one of those words came from the prophet's own mind, but every single one was inspired by the Holy Spirit.

2 Even so, there were also *false* prophets in Israel, just as there will be false teachers among you. They will try to slide some devastating heresies by you, and many people will be sucked in by them. But make no mistake, these false teachers, and those who follow them, are headed for doom and destruction. What other destiny could possibly await one who denies the Lord and jeers at His ways? They are greedy for control and they want to exert power for their own gain. If you let them, they'll take advantage of you using their knack for deception. But God's not asleep at the wheel, and their time for judgment has been appointed.

Think about it this way. If God didn't spare the rebellious angels from the judgment that awaited their sin, if God didn't spare the world from the punishment of its sin in the days of Noah, if God didn't spare Sodom and Gomorrah when they flaunted their flagrant immorality, then He will surely have a judgment in store for these evildoers, too. Those rebellious angels were cast down to hell and delivered into chains of darkness, Noah's world was met with a judgment of total destruction by global flood, and Sodom and Gomorrah were made to be an example when God wiped them off the map. Yet Noah and his family were saved, as were Lot and his family. (They had been oppressed by the wicked because of their righteousness. Indeed, it was a source of torment to Lot to have to live among those people and constantly observe their wicked behavior.) What does all this tell us? That the Lord knows how to keep godly people from being overtaken by ungodly people.

But judgment is coming for the ungodly. Particularly these false teachers who just do whatever they want, even embracing sexual immorality and rebuffing the authorities God has placed over them. They are audacious and arrogant, and they think nothing of badmouthing what angels won't even dare to judge. They rail against things they don't understand. They're like wild animals that look powerful and scary but don't have the wisdom to avoid the trap. Their own sin will catch and destroy them.

Their idea of a good time is to get drunk and disorderly in the middle of the day. They are soft and given to the finer things, moral blemishes and disgraces to the true people of God. During your fellowship meals, when the Church is rightly enjoying holy community, these narcissists are eating and drinking to excess, and deceiving anyone they can into serving their own selfish purposes. Their eyes are full of adultery. They simply refuse to stop committing sin. And they bring down all the weaker people around them, too. They've trained their hearts—whether actively or passively—to want what others have.

They've made a choice to abandon what they know to be right and pursue what they know to be wrong. They're like Balaam, son of Beor, in that respect. He foolishly cashed the paycheck of wickedness, but in the end it was he who paid the price. His own donkey had more brains than he did, prophetically speaking to him the sense he would have possessed himself if he hadn't been the kind of prophet who relinquishes his own spiritual sanity.

These people are wells without water and clouds whose instability shows every time the storm winds gust. They have earned the wages of unrighteousness. They are children of the curse. The pitch-black world of eternal darkness is reserved for them.

Their speech is pretentious and devoid of worthwhile content. Yet, the way they deliberately pander to the lusts of those poor souls who are hanging on to the truth by a thread, they are as enchanting as the Sirens. They say they're preaching Christian liberty, but they're actually inviting into their lives a cruel slavemaster called *sin* who has the stench of death all over him. Make no mistake, you're a slave to whatever controls you. And if you're one of the ones who came to know Jesus as Lord and found an escape from the world's wickedness, yet you let yourself get duped into falling right back into this evil slavemaster's control, you're worse off than before. It would be far better to go through life without ever walking the path of righteousness than it would be to find the path and then turn away from it. But these sad people epitomize the proverbs: "A dog returns to its own vomit," and "A pig goes back to wallowing in the mud right after it's washed."

3 Look, this is the second letter I've written to you. And in both, because I believe in the purity of your faith, I've tried to remind you and inspire you to rehearse the words of the old prophets and the commandments of the new apostles, which together herald the same message: Jesus graciously saves everyone who submits to Him as Lord. Keeping this truth before you at all times is so important, because in the last days, self-serving scoffers will come around and try to sow seeds of doubt. They'll say things like, "Is He really coming? Did He really promise that He would? It doesn't seem like it's going to happen. Everything's pretty much the same as it always has been from the beginning." Because they're not of the ones who rehearse the fundamentals of the faith, they willfully forget God made the heavens and the earth by His Word, He brought forth the land out of the water by His Word, and He destroyed that same earth by covering it back up with water. And now the heavens and the earth are being preserved by His Word until Judgment Day, when His fire will destroy the ungodly.

Friends, don't fall for the deception. Remember that with the Lord a day is as a thousand years and a thousand years is as a day. The reason He delays His coming is not that He's reneging on His promise, it's that He is so loving and merciful that He wants to give people as much time as possible to take Him up on His offer of forgiveness. He doesn't want anyone to miss out and be destroyed. His preference is that every single person would repent.

Nevertheless, the Day of the Lord will come, stealthily and unexpectedly, like a thief in the night. The sky will be rolled back like a scroll, causing a noise of massive proportion. Everything in the universe will be exposed to the heat of the Refiner's fire. As everything melts, the impurities of the earth and all of its endeavors will be exposed for what they are. Therefore, since nothing will escape the fire of God, you'd better make sure you're living holy, godly lives, knowing that only what is of God will survive such a purging. In fact, our holy conduct actually serves to accelerate His coming. And we will hold onto the promise of a new heaven and new earth, where only righteousness is allowed to live.

So, friends, let's be looking forward to all of these things, doing everything within our power to remain spotless and blameless in His sight. Keep in mind that the Lord's patience in this season results in the salvation of souls. Our dear brother, Paul, from an inspiration of divine wisdom, wrote the same thing in his letters. (Some of the things he wrote can be a bit hard to understand, and if you get the wrong kind of person interpreting them, they can twist his words into a heresy that will destroy them and the people they teach. Then again, that type of person is going to twist everything in the Bible that way.)

Friends, I've written these things to you so that you will really get it into your skulls ahead of time to stay on guard. That way as times grow more precarious, you won't shrink back from being steadfast in the faith, you won't be led away by the lies of the wicked, but rather you'll grow in the grace of our Lord and Savior Jesus Christ, knowing Him more and more intimately. Glory be to Him, now and forever. Amen.

Earnestly,
Simon Peter, a slave and apostle of Jesus Christ

THE LETTER FROM
JUDE

To my dear spiritual siblings who are under the watchful care of Jesus Christ, called of God, made holy by our Father in heaven,

May the mercy, peace, and love of God increase within you more and more.

Friends, I wanted to write you about our salvation, but instead I feel it's necessary to urge you to put up a valiant fight in defense of the faith, the one *true* faith that is the same for all people for all time. There are some who have infiltrated the ranks of Christendom who have no business being with you. Here's how you'll know who I'm talking about: they want to stretch the grace of Christ to the point where it allows for blatant immorality, and in particular, a shameless lack of sexual restraint. They want to claim Jesus as Savior without claiming Him as Master. It doesn't work that way! You have to do what He says! Since they don't, their guilty verdict was already pronounced a long time ago.

Think about these historic episodes as a backdrop to the current situation (I know you already know these stories, but receive them again as a sober reminder):

1) The same God who delivered His people out of Egypt turned right around and wiped a bunch of them out. Why? Because they didn't believe and obey!

2) There was a whole cohort of angels who had it made in the shade, living a life of wonder in the presence of God, even carrying a degree of authority. And they gave it all

up to pursue their own prideful pleasures. Now what? God has relegated them to utter darkness, keeping them chained up until Judgment Day, when they will get the ultimate smack down.

3) Sodom and Gomorrah, and the other towns around them, debased themselves, practicing extreme immorality and sexual perversion. And God made an example out of them by making them suffer the punishment of eternal fire.

Now consider the characters you're dealing with in light of these examples. They are giving themselves over to evil fantasies. They incur defilement by their sinful practices, they rebel against authority, and they speak disparagingly of those who actually bring glory to God. Are you kidding me?! Michael, the archangel, didn't even speak against the *devil* in that fashion. (That was when they were arguing about the body of Moses.) Instead, he was content to simply say, "The *Lord* rebuke you." But no, these people badmouth things they haven't even understood. And the things they do understand they only understand according to their worldly perspectives; that will be the death of them. "Hell's comin', punks! You've got murderous hearts of hate like Cain, you've got greedy intentions like Balaam, and you're as rebellious as Korah! You don't stand a chance!"

These people are trying to come participate in your fellowship meals?! Believer beware! It's clear they're only out for themselves. They are hidden icebergs in the black of night, and you are the Titanic! They are as useless as a cloud without water, and just as unstable. They're trees without fruit, even though the fruit should be in season; when you look closer, you'll find they've actually been uprooted. They're rogue stars headed for eternal darkness. They're rough and headstrong ocean waves, and the foam they churn up is shamefulness.

Enoch, the seventh-generation descendant of Adam, prophesied about them. "The Lord is coming with multitudes of His saints, to try, convict, and sentence every person who has practiced unrighteousness. Yes, every blasphemous word that His enemies have spoken against Him will be met with justice!"

These people level complaints against God in their own hearts and minds. They do only what satisfies their own corrupt cravings. They will flatter you to your face if it will get them what they want. Friends, keep in mind what the Lord's apostles told you before. They told you that in the last days there would be scoffers who would continually fulfill their own ungodly lusts. These are divisive, carnally minded people who do not have the Spirit.

But you, my dear brothers and sisters, you be sure to stay firmly planted in the love of God, building yourself up in faith by praying in the Holy Spirit. Posture yourself to receive a daily dose of mercy from the Lord Jesus Christ until you have laid claim to that precious gift of eternal life.

Now, be wise in your dealings with people. Not everyone who sins is of the same ilk I've been describing. Some are merely misguided and need someone to compassionately walk them through restoration. Others are on the brink of disaster and need to be yanked out of the fire by any-and-all means. Let the Holy Spirit show you how to discern these things properly.

Now to Him who is willing and able to keep you from stumbling, and to happily present you without fault before the presence of His glory; to God our Savior, the only Source of all wisdom; be glory and majesty, power and authority, now and forevermore. Amen.

Emphatically,
Jude, slave of Jesus Christ, brother of James

Discussion Questions

WEEK 20: 2 Peter & Jude

- Peter lays out a progression of Christian growth in the opening of his second letter (1:5-7). Where do you think you are in the progression? What do you need to do to keep moving forward?
- Chapter 2 reveals the impetus for the letter: false teachers. Their kind is clearly marked by selfishness, and sexual immorality is a clue to their identity. Discuss the zero-tolerance policy Peter has (and God has) toward these people.
- Reflect on the "Day of the Lord" that Peter describes in Chapter 3, and note in particular the "therefore" that explains how we should be preparing ourselves for it.
- Discuss the similarities between Jude and 2 Peter 2.

ACKNOWLEDGEMENTS

The moral support and logistical support All Peoples Ministries has given me made this book possible. Thank you, Jeff and Sam!

As always, my chief proofreader was my mom, Nell. Thanks for the time and effort, Mom. Great work!

In addition, I would like to thank all the others who read and gave feedback on this project, including the members of All Peoples Church. In particular, several Bible-savvy veterans were called upon to go through and make sure there was nothing afoul. (God knows that being faithful to the true essence of His Word was of primary importance to me!) So, thank you to the hermeneutics police: Pastor Bud Crawford, Jeffrey Crawford, Dr. Samantha Miller, and Nell Miller.

www.ingramcontent.com/pod-product-compliance
Lightning Source LLC
Chambersburg PA
CBHW051825090426

42736CB00011B/1645